THE TRADITIO
AGA
BOOK OF
SLOW
COOKING

THE TRADITIONAL
AGA
BOOK OF
SLOW
COOKING

Louise Walker

ABSOLUTE PRESS

First published in 1997 by Absolute Press, Scarborough House,
29 James Street West, Bath, BA1 2BT. Tel: 01225 316013 Fax: 01225 445836
email sales@absolutepress.co.uk

Reprinted January 1998
Reprinted January 1999
Reprinted January 2001
Reprinted November 2001
Reprinted April 2002
Reprinted December 2002
Reprinted December 2003

ISBN 1 899791 21 3

Cover and text Design by Ian Middleton
Cover and text illustrations by Caroline Nisbett

Printed by Butler & Tanner Ltd, Frome and London
Covers printed by Lawrence-Allen Ltd, Weston-Super-Mare

CONTENTS

GENERAL
INTRODUCTION

CONVERSION CHART

This is the metric/imperial conversion chart that I have used. Do keep to either metric or imperial measures throughout the whole recipe. Mixing the two can lead to all kinds of problems. Eggs used in testing have been size 3. Tablespoon and teaspoon measures have been level unless otherwise stated.

25g	1 oz
50g	2 oz
75g	3 oz
100g	4 oz
150g	5 oz
175g	6 oz
200g	7 oz
225g	8 oz
250g	9 oz
275g	10 oz
300g	11 oz
350g	12 oz
375g	13 oz
400g	14 oz
425g	15 oz
450g	16 oz (1 lb)
5ml	1 tsp
15ml	1 tbsp
150ml	$^1/_4$ pint
300ml	$^1/_2$ pint
450ml	$^3/_4$ pint
600ml	1 pint
20cm tin	8 inch tin

AN INTRODUCTION TO SLOW COOKING

Everyone knows that Agas are brilliant for one thing – cooking food slowly. They are of course good for all other cooking methods, quick stir-fries, perfect pastry, moist cakes let alone drying the washing and more besides.

But back to slow cooking. The gentle even heat of the simmering oven cooks food at an even temperature with little moisture loss, so casseroles, cakes and puddings will cook at an even pace and come out luscious and moist. Food cooking in the simmering oven will not dry out and spoil if it is not taken out at the precise time stated in the recipe, and, as all Aga-owners know, it is easy to leave food cooking longer than planned because no smells permeate the kitchen! I admit to having left stock and meringues in the simmering oven for at least three days! Although the food may be still edible and not totally spoilt after long cooking in the simmering oven, the flavours will not be at their peak, meat will be too soft and vegetables may be mushy, so I have tried to give the optimum cooking time as tested on my two-oven gas-fired Aga. All Agas are different: for example I find that simmering ovens on the four-oven Agas tend to be cooler than my two-oven simmering oven and of course Agas converted to a second fuel very often have simmering ovens of very variable temperatures. After a couple of test recipes do be prepared to adjust cooking times to suit your Aga. Where appropriate, I have given the cooking times and electric oven temperatures for some recipes for the benefit of those not yet owning an Aga! These recipes have been tested on a non-fan mode of an electric oven which seems most appropriate for slow cooking. If you are cooking in an electric oven do keep an eye on the dish as there is more tendency for liquids to evaporate in an electric oven than an Aga. A really tight-fitting lid to the casserole dish will help.

There are a few rules to be followed when using the simmering oven. Apart from meringues, rich fruit cakes and porridge, food to be cooked at this lower temperature needs to be heated before it will cook in the simmering oven. Either heat the food on the simmering plate for 5 minutes to make sure the food and the cooking pot are hot all the way through before transferring to the simmering oven; or put the dish in the roasting oven for 15-30 minutes until bubbling hot.This latter method is best if your chosen casserole dish is not flameproof or if, for some reason, your oven temperature is low. Shelf positions don't matter in the simmering oven — it all depends upon what else you will be cooking at the same time. Cover food with a lid or foil to prevent drying out on the surface and a crust forming. Remember that filling the oven will lower the temperature, so allow extra time if you plan to cook for a large crowd.

A word about re-heating: casseroles, curries etc often have a better flavour if cooked a day in advance and then reheated. All hot food should be served piping hot, so reheat either in the roasting oven or on the simmering plate until not just bubbling but really hot. At this stage the dish can be held in the simmering oven if you are not quite ready to serve.

I hope this book gives you some fresh ideas for dishes that can be popped in the oven at the beginning of the day and left to cook slowly without you standing over them; and to serve with the minimum of fuss at the last minute.

GENERAL INTRODUCTION

....

I know from the demonstrating and workshop sessions I run, that there are two types of Aga owner: those who choose an Aga to put into their home and those who inherit an Aga when they move house. The former have either been brought up with an Aga, or they have had the opportunity to observe the multitude of benefits bestowed by the presence of an Aga. The latter are often terrified by the great monster in the kitchen, but after only a few months, the fear has gone and they are quite converted.

We all love the constant warmth when the Aga is on, creating that heart to the kitchen. I have yet to find an Aga owner, new or old, who would change to another cooker, let alone give up all those other conveniences the Aga provides. The most popular selling Agas at the moment are gas-fired. However, not so long ago solid fuel was the popular fuel for Agas and some people still think that Agas can only be properly run on this. In fact many other fuels can be used: electricity, liquid propane, gas and oil.

The solid fuel Agas are the most complicated to run and, if yours is one of those, your own experience will tell you how to fuel it for the particular cooking task in hand. Fortunately this experience does not take long to acquire. As with all Agas, keep the lids down as much as possible; some people open the vent door to give an extra boost of heat during cooking. Agas converted from solid fuel to oil or gas often have personality differences. For example, the ovens may prove difficult to regulate for various recipes. However, personality differences are fairly typical of all Agas, as they are made individually and are sited and fuelled differently.

Like all new kitchen appliances, it takes time to get to know your Aga; perhaps this is the secret of the great Aga-owners' loyalty – it becomes a personality in the kitchen. However, all this does mean that writing recipes for an Aga can in no way be regarded as an exact science. Almost everything should be treated as guidelines. I hope that the recipes in this book will give you ideas on the efficient use of your Aga and on its range of capabilities. You can then go on to experiment confidently with other recipes.

LOOKING AFTER YOUR AGA

....

If you are doing a lot of cooking or entertaining, for example, at Christmas, turn up the Aga a little more than usual. If you are used to the chore of cleaning a gas or electric cooker, you will love the simplicity of keeping the Aga clean. Mine gets a thorough clean just once a year, when it is switched off for servicing; mine is gas-fired, an oil-fired one needs 6-monthly servicing. The night before servicing I switch off the Aga completely. After the breakfast is cleared away I set to on the cleaning and try to do as much as possible before the engineer arrives. Remove everything possible; the oven shelves and the doors which simply lift off. Brush out all the carbon deposits from the ovens. Anything still sticky on the floor of the oven can be removed with a wooden spatula, and the remains left to carbonise.

Clean the lids of the boiling plate, simmering plate and round the inside of the oven door frames with a warm soapy cloth and a paste cleaner such as Astonish. Never be tempted to use a wire wool pad or a tough abrasive. Some elbow grease may be needed but you will be surprised how much dirt will come off. Rinse off with a clean cloth and buff up. Clean the oven shelves in a sink of soapy water and more Astonish if needed. Wipe round the doors and clean the inside of the top and lower oven doors if necessary. The other doors will probably not get dirty. If you are concerned about the state of the seals remember to get the engineer to check them. Return all the bits and pieces to their places and give the whole Aga a wipe down and buff up. I know some people who polish their Agas occasionally! Other than the annual clean; try to wipe up any spills as they occur and wipe off any other crumbs, dust and so on daily. I find a lot of dust on my Aga, partly due to all the laundry put to dry or air above it.

POTS, PANS AND ACCESSORIES

Many people worry about their saucepans when they have a new Aga. If they are looked after, new pans purchased with an Aga will last a lifetime because there is no warping of the bases due to the even heat area. However, it isn't always necessary to rush out and buy pans. Think carefully about what you need and buy one at a time.

If you have existing pans there are two ways of testing their suitability for the Aga. Turn the pan upside down and put a ruler or something with a straight edge across the base. If daylight shows through; the pan will not work efficiently. Alternatively half-fill the pan with water and put on the boiling plate to boil. If only a poor contact is being made the water will not boil. Beware — even toast crumbs on the plate can have the same effect. A good, heavy-based pan is best. The size, shape and metal varies so choose according to your personal needs and preferences. Pans that go on the hot plates and in the oven are very useful. The Aga showroom will have a good range to show you.

A kettle is useful, as your Aga is on all the time and always ready to boil water, but the shape and style are your own personal preference. Choose a heavy base and ask if you can do a water pouring test in the showroom or shop so that you know that the kettle suits you.

The Aga tins are useful because they fit the runners of the oven and can be used as shelves. The roasting rack for the tins are handy to use when roasting fatty meat, or for grilling bacon, sausages and chops.

You will use ovenproof dishes quite a lot because so much cooking is done in the ovens. I find pans and casseroles that can be used on the top plates and in the oven especially useful but beware, wooden or plastic handles as those on the Agaluxe range cannot be used in the roasting oven. In time wooden handles will dry out and come apart. Cast-iron pans and dishes are useful for their multi-purpose use but they can be heavy to lift!

COOKING WITH THE AGA

The Aga uses stored heat, and the ovens cook really well when they are evenly heated, so the aim is to cook with as little heat loss as possible. As soon as the hot plate lids are raised, heat will be lost, so use the ovens as much as possible. Of course, that way all the smells and condensation go up the chimney.

To maintain heat, the heavy insulated lids are kept down when the hot plate is not in use. The shiny lids are slightly domed. Do not be tempted to put the kettle or other pots and pans on the lid without using a protective pad — once scratched always scratched. Always remember — as soon as cooking is finished put the lids down so that heat is restored.

Frying, steaming and grilling can be done in the oven, while toast is done in the 'bat' on the boiling plate.

The ovens, which look so small from the outside, are very spacious inside. Aga roasting tins are designed to fit exactly so they will slide on the runners without the use of the oven shelf. Agas are now supplied with a roasting tin with racks to fit. The rack makes a useful cooling rack when you are doing a lot of baking. Two oven shelves with useful anti-tilt devices are also supplied. If you have the opportunity, try sliding the shelves in and out of the oven before the Aga is fired up. They are easy to use once you have the knack, but difficult to manage when hot if you have not tried it before. I know one couple who spent a whole day trying to get their shelves out!

The mysterious cold plain shelf is also supplied. This also fits the runners and can be used as an oven shelf or a baking tray. However, it should be kept out of the oven, somewhere cool, so that it can be used to diffuse the heat when the hot oven is used to cook foods at a lower temperature. I met one lady, an Aga owner for 30 years, who did not know what the cold plain shelf was really for. No wonder she thought my demonstration was a revelation!

TIPS AND USES FOR THE AGA

One of the best tips I can give when buying a Aga is to buy a timer you can carry around with you! There are no smells from the Aga oven, so it is easy to forget about food cooking inside. I think all Aga owners have opened the oven and thought "what was that lump of charcoal?" Those yellow sticky note pads are useful – reminders on the breakfast table to "remember porridge" or "remember stock/Christmas cakes/puddings etc". I have been known to put a reminder "remember casserole" on my pillow so that I remove it before going to bed.

Dry baking tins and awkwardly shaped cooking utensils on top of the Aga – there are no excuses for rusty tins.

Pastry cases for quiches do not need to be baked blind. Simply cook them directly on the floor of the roasting oven for a crisp base. It is safe to use porcelain, glass and metal flan dishes.

Stand mugs of tea or coffee on top of the Aga to keep warm when the telephone rings.

To defrost cakes or bread, stand them on top of the simmering plate lid or place in the simmering oven.

Dry the washing on top of the simmering plate lid – the boiling plate is too hot. Spin the items to be dried, smooth out any creases and lay on the lid – no ironing needed! Hang towels or sheets over the chrome rail – just take care not to cover the air vents on the control box door.

If your kitchen ceiling is high enough, a kitchen maid above the Aga is useful for drying washing. Hang dried flowers on the ends so that it does not look too utilitarian.

Rugby boots washed of all their mud, and washed trainers, can be hung by their laces on the chrome rail and dried.

Shoes wet from winter rain should be stuffed full with newspaper and dried in front of the Aga – the gentle heat will not spoil the leather.

When the snow comes the Aga heat is busy not just producing hot food but drying snowy gloves and socks, as well as warming coats, hats and boots.

Finally, a word about oven gloves. Go for the long Aga gauntlets: no more burnt arms reaching to the back of the oven to get that elusive dish or potato.

BASIC AGA TECHNIQUES

FISH

Although there are no recipes in this book for slow-cooked fish, I have included this basic guide as cooking fish in the Aga is so easy and cuts out fishy smells! The variety of fish available is increasing all the time, so experiment with different fish and different cooking methods. I have given approximate cooking times, but this will depend upon the size and thickness of the fish. Try not to overcook as this gives dry, stringy, tasteless fish.

POACHING FISH

Place the fish in the roasting tin, cover with water, wine or milk, add salt, pepper and a bayleaf. Hang the tin on the third set of runners from the top of the roasting oven for 15-20 minutes.

POACHING WHOLE LARGE FISH

Clean the fish. Sprinkle with salt if desired, and wrap in buttered foil, sealing well. Lift the parcel into the roasting tin, pour boiling water into the tin to come half-way up the fish. Hang on the second set of runners from the top of the roasting oven. Cook for 10 minutes per lb (450g), turning the fish half-way through cooking. Remove from the oven and allow to cool. Serve warm or remove the skin when cold.

FRIED FISH

Wash and dry the fish. If required, coat it with seasoned flour, batter, oatmeal or egg and fresh breadcrumbs. Put enough cooking oil into the roasting tin to coat the base. Put the tin on the floor of the roasting oven and heat until hazing. Add the fish and continue to cook on the floor of the oven. Turn the fish half-way through the cooking time.

GRILLED FISH

Lay fish cutlets in a roasting tin, brush with oil and seasoning. Hang the tin on the highest set of runners and grill, turning half-way through the cooking time. It sometimes rings the changes to marinade the fish for half an hour and grill with the grill rack in the roasting tin, basting or brushing with a little more marinade part-way through cooking. This will give a more charred appearance and taste.

ROASTING MEAT

Meat roasted in the Aga will be moist and flavoursome. Only a smearing of extra fat is needed to start the cooking. Season as you prefer — salt, pepper, fresh herbs etc. If the meat is stuffed do this and then weigh to calculate cooking times. There are two methods of roasting using the Aga. The Quick Roasting Method is the more traditional method, used for more tender cuts of meat. The Slow Roasting Method is best for less fine cuts of meat.

QUICK ROASTING METHOD

Season the meat and put in the Aga roasting tin. Stand on the grill rack if you like. Hang the tin on the middle set of runners of the roasting oven for the calculated time. Baste with hot fat periodically. The shape of the joint will also affect the cooking time — a long narrow joint will not take so long as a short, fat joint. When the meat is cooked, allow the joint to rest in the simmering oven for 15 minutes before carving. This is useful time to make gravy and cook last minute green vegetables.

SLOW COOKING METHOD

Season and prepare the meat as above. Put the roasting tin into the roasting oven on the middle set of runners for 30 minutes or until the meat is browning and getting hot. Then transfer to the simmering oven, and cook for twice the time calculated for the normal roasting method.

TIMES FOR ROASTING:

Roast beef:	
rare	10 minutes per lb/450g plus 10 minutes
medium	15 minutes per lb/450g plus 15 minutes
well done	20 minutes per lb/450g plus 20 minutes
Fillet	10 minutes per lb/450g plus 10 minutes
Roast pork:	30 minutes per lb/450g plus 30 minutes
Lamb:	
pink	15 minutes per lb/450g plus 15 minutes
medium	20 minutes per lb/450g plus 20 minutes
Veal:	20 minutes per lb/450g plus 20 minutes

ROASTING POULTRY AND GAME

Roast poultry and game from the Aga will produce crisp skin on the outside of moist tender flesh. A lot of Aga owners like to cook their large turkey overnight in the simmering oven. It is advisable to start the turkey in the hot roasting oven for at least 45 minutes before moving to the simmering oven. This ensures the meat is hot. Finish the cooking by moving the bird to the roasting oven for the final half-hour.

Smear the bird with a little butter. Put bacon rashers over the breast if liked. Stand on the rack in the roasting tin. Put lemon or herbs in the body cavity if liked. Hang the tin on the middle set of runners for the following times.

ROASTING TIMES
(IN THE ROASTING OVEN)

Bird	Weight	Approx. cooking times
Chicken	2lb/900g	45–50 minutes
	3lb/1.5kg	1 hour
	4lb/1.75kg	$1^1/_2$ hour
	5lb/2.25kg	$1^3/_4$ hours
Turkey	8-10lb/3.5–4.5kg	$1^3/_4$–2 hours
	11-15lb/5–7.25kg	$2^1/_2$ hours
	16-22lb/7.5–10kg	3 hours
Duck		$1–1^1/_2$ hours
Goose		$1^1/_2$–2 hours
Grouse		30–35 minutes
Pigeon		20–35 minutes
Partridge		30–35 minutes
Pheasant		45–50 minutes
Quail		15 minutes
Snipe		15 minutes
Woodcock		15 minutes

To test if cooked: pierce the thickest part of the thigh with a fine skewer, if the juices run clear the bird is cooked. Allow the bird to rest in the simmering oven whilst making gravy from the skimmed cooking juices.

BOILED BACON AND GAMMON JOINTS

....

Cooking a whole piece of ham in the Aga is so easy and gives a moist joint, perfect for slicing. I even cook ham for friends because they love the moistness and really it takes very little effort.

Soak the joint in water for 2–3 hours to remove any saltiness. Put a trivet or an old saucer in the bottom of a suitably sized pan. Put the joint on top and pour in enough cold water to come 2–3 inches up the side of the pan. Cover. Stand on the simmering plate and bring slowly to the boil and simmer for 30 minutes. Transfer the joint to the simmering oven for the following times:

2–3 lb/900g–1.5kg	2½ hours
4–5 lb/1.75–2.25kg	3 hours
6–7 lb/2.75–3 kg	3½ hours
8–9 lb/3.5–4 kg	4½ hours
10–11 lb/4.5–5kg	5½ hours
12–13 lb/5.5–6kg	6½ hours
14–15 lb/6.5–6.75kg	7½ hours
16 lb/7.25 kg and over	overnight

Remove the pan from the oven and lift out the joint. Cool a little to handle. Strip off the skin and score the fat. Mix together a glaze of mustard and honey and spread over the surface. Stud with cloves if liked. Stand in a roasting tin with the glazing uppermost. Hang the tin so that the meat is in the middle of the roasting oven and bake for 10–20 minutes, until a golden glaze has formed. Watch it closely, it may burn! Serve hot or cold.

THICKENINGS

....

There are a variety of ways of thickening soups, stews and casseroles. The thickness of the gravy is largely a matter of personal taste, but also bear in mind what is to accompany the dish.

As an emergency thickener when time is short, a few instant thickening granuals can save the day. Keep a tub handy in the cupboard.

Cornflour is an easy and much used way of thickening at the end of cooking. Remember to 'slake' the cornflour with some water to make a smooth paste before adding to the hot food. Adding a little of the hot gravy to the cornflour also helps the blending process. Boil the casserole either on the simmering plate or in the oven for a few minutes until thickened.

Arrowroot is used in the same way as cornflour, but it will give a clearer, less cloudy finish to the gravy.

Reducing through boiling and then stirring in a knob of butter gives a glossy gravy, but never so thick as a gravy thickened with cornflour. Always strain the gravy off from the meat and vegetables before boiling so that the other ingredients are not spoilt by boiling. Boil the gravy rapidly to reduce to the required consistency. Whisk in a knob of butter at the end and pour over the meat and vegetables.

Buerre manié is a traditional French way to thicken gravies that gives a thickened, glossy sauce. Work together 1 tablespoon butter and 1 dessertspoon flour to make a paste. Drop small pieces of this mixture into the gravy and stir well whilst allowing to bubble gently on the simmering plate.

BOILED POTATOES AND OTHER ROOT VEGETABLES

Potatoes, along with other root vegetables, are best cooked in a slow oven. This both conserves the stored heat in the Aga and prevents the kitchen filling with steam. You will need to use a pan that can be used on the hot plate and in the oven simmering, so no wooden handles. Do not be tempted to transfer the potatoes to a cold serving dish part-way through cooking – the entire heat of the pan, water and vegetables is needed for successful cooking.

Wash and prepare the potatoes in the usual way. Cut them to an even size. Place in the pan, add salt to taste and add about 2.5cm (1 inch) water. Cover and bring to the boil on the plate, boil for 1–2 minutes, drain off the water and then transfer to the simmering oven. It is difficult to give timings, as the cooking time will depend upon the type and size of potato.

Allow 30 minutes and then test. Small new potatoes and small pieces of root vegetable will take about 20 minutes. Drain the vegetables, toss in butter if liked, and serve or return to the pan and the oven to keep warm.

ROASTING VEGETABLES

Roast vegetables are always a great favourite. I know that it is fashionably healthy to eat baked potatoes instead of roast, and steamed instead of roast parsnips, but nothing beats roast vegetables with roast meat for a special treat.

Peel and cut the vegetables to an even size. Boil for 1 minute in salted water, then drain thoroughly. While the vegetables are draining and drying put some cooking oil, lard or dripping into the roasting tin. Slide onto the floor of the roasting oven. When the fat is hot tip in the dry vegetables, toss them in the fat and return to the oven, hanging the tin on one of the runners. If you are also roasting meat it may be necessary to juggle the tins during cooking. Cooking near the top will give an evenly cooked, crispy vegetable. Putting on the floor of the oven will crisp the bottom of the vegetables well. Vegetables take about 1 hour to roast. If the vegetables are put around the meat they may take longer and are often not so crispy, but they do taste wonderful!

RICE

A lot of people seem to have trouble cooking rice. Cooked in the oven of the Aga, it is very simple and can be kept hot without spoiling if you want to cook the rice slightly in advance. This is the basic method for cooking rice. Adjust the quantities to suit your needs. Use a saucepan that is happy both on the hot plate and in the oven.

1 cup rice
1 1/2 cups water
good pinch salt

Wash the rice in a sieve with cold, running water. Put in the saucepan. Add salt and water. Put on the lid.

Bring to the boil on the boiling plate. When boiling, transfer to the simmering oven. Cook for the appropriate time. The times I have given produce a cooked, non-soggy rice. If you like your rice a little more cooked, then leave it in the oven for a little longer.

Remove the pan from the oven and drain the rice through a sieve — some types of rice will have absorbed all the water. If liked, rinse with boiling water. Serve.

Alternatively if you want to keep the rice hot, return to the pan and stir in a small knob of butter. Cover and return to the bottom oven until needed.

COOKING TIMES:

White long-grain rice	12 minutes
Brown long-grain rice	20 minutes
Basmati rice	10 minutes

PASTA

Pasta needs a fast boil when cooking to prevent it sticking together. Try to use a pan that is deeper than its width. Half-fill with water, add salt to taste, cover and bring to the boil on the boiling plate. Add the pasta, fresh or dried, cover and bring to the boil — watch, this will not take long! Remove the lid and start timing according to the packet instructions. Alternativley transfer to one of the ovens. When the pasta comes to the boil, start timing. When al dente, drain through a colander, return to the pan and toss in a little oil or butter to prevent sticking. Serve straight away with a chosen sauce.

DRIED BEANS AND PEAS

The range of dried beans available in the shops gives a whole host of flavours, colours and textures for cooking. The beans and other grains can be used for vegetarian cooking or to make meat dishes go further or just to add variety. Lentils do not need soaking before cooking, just washing and picking over. All the other pulses need to be washed, picked over and left to soak for 8–12 hours or overnight — so some forethought is necessary.

Measure out the pulses required, wash well and pick over to remove any grit. Place in a bowl and cover with cold water. Put aside to soak.

Drain the liquid from the beans. Place in a saucepan, cover with cold water and bring to the boil. Boil rapidly for 10 minutes – to prevent boiling over use a large pan and no lid at this stage. After 10 minutes of rapid boiling, cover and transfer to the simmering oven until tender, 1–3 hours. The length of time depends upon the type and age of the bean. Experience will be your best judge. When cooked, use as per recipe.

PORRIDGE

We love porridge in the winter and it is a great favourite with a variety of toppings. I have to say that lashings of soft brown sugar comes top of the list, though I like fruit or salt – my husband favours yoghurt. This is the easiest breakfast dish to prepare, though if you are an infrequent maker of porridge you may need to leave a reminder on the breakfast table that some is in the oven! I have given a recipe for four servings, but I do know some people who make individual portions in a small cereal bowl with a saucer on top as a lid.

1 cup rolled porridge oats
1 cup water
1 cup milk
pinch salt

Put all the ingredients into a small saucepan, cover, and put in the simmering oven overnight. Stir and serve with milk or cream and your favourite flavouring.

PRESERVES

....

Home-made jams and chutneys are easy to make, though a little time consuming. Quite a lot of the cooking can be done in the simmering oven. This removes the need to watch the preserving pan all the time and prevents burning on the bottom of the pan. Jams or chutneys make wonderful presents, particularly when presented with an attractive label or in a pretty jar.

I am giving an outline for basic methods of preservation. For more detail HMSO publish *Home Preservation of Fruit and Vegetables* which is a really good reference book. Alternatively, my few recipes will give you the basic method and other recipes can be used. A good, large preserving pan will be needed. I use a large deep catering pan with a lid. With mine I can get the jam boiling well without too much spitting. The lid is useful when cooking slowly in the low oven. Collect jam jars with good, clean lids. I put mine through the dishwasher and keep them ready with their lids on. They only need warming in the lower oven when needed. Labels and wax discs are needed.

When making jam or marmalade here are a few basic tips: some fruit that needs slightly longer cooking, for instance, apricots, can be cooked in the simmering oven until softened. Choose granulated or preserving sugar and always make sure it is dissolved before bringing to the boil, to prevent crystallising.

To test for set, remove the boiling jam from the heat after 10–15 minutes rapid boil. Put about 1 teaspoon of jam on a cold plate. Chill the sample for 1–2 minutes. If the surface wrinkles when pushed with the finger, the setting point has been reached. If the setting point has not been reached, boil again for 2–3 minutes and re-test. Too much boiling will give a syrupy jam. Cool the jam in the pan for a few minutes to prevent fruit rising to the top of the jar. Put the wax discs and lids on when the jam is either first put in the jar or when cold. Clean and label the jars when cold. Store in a cool, dark place.

SOUPS AND STARTERS

SOUPS AND STARTERS

Soups cook beautifully in the simmering oven. The basis of a good soup is a good stock which is made so easily in the Aga. This stock can of course be used for casseroles wherever stock is called for.

MEAT AND GAME STOCKS

Place the bones in a large saucepan with 2 or 3 flavouring vegetables, such as onions, celery and carrots. Add some peppercorns and a bouquet garni. Just cover with cold water and bring to the boil on the boiling plate. Skim any residue from the top. Simmer for about 10 minutes and then transfer to the simmering oven for 8–10 hours or overnight. Remove from the oven and strain through a sieve. Store the clear stock in the fridge or freeze in useful sizes.

VEGETABLE STOCK

Wash and chop a selection of vegetables. Place in a saucepan and add some peppercorns and a bouquet garni. Just cover with water and bring to the boil. Simmer for 10 minutes, then transfer to the simmering oven for 3–4 hours. Strain and discard the vegetables. Store in the fridge or freeze for later use.

Of course there are times when we all use stock cubes or powder. When seasoning the finished dish remember that these commercial stocks tend to be very salty, so season with care.

CREAM OF CHICKEN SOUP

This soup is a meal in itself. Any left-over chicken can be used for another dish, e.g. stuffed pancakes, pies etc.

1 small chicken, about 1kg/2 lb 4 oz
1 large onion, chopped
2 celery stalks chopped
2 large carrots, sliced
1 leek, sliced
bouquet garni
blade of mace
rind and juice of 1 lemon
salt and pepper
40g/1¹/₂ oz butter
40g/1¹/₂ oz flour
2 egg yolks
150ml/¹/₄ pint double cream

Put the chicken and vegetables into a large flameproof casserole. Add the bouquet garni, mace, lemon rind and juice, salt and pepper. Add enough water to just cover the chicken. Stand on the boiling plate and bring to the boil. Skim off any scum and transfer to the simmering oven and cook for 1¹/₂–2 hours, or until the chicken is tender.

Remove the chicken and take the meat off the carcass. For the soup you will need 225–350g (8–12 oz) meat. Strain the stock and reserve about 1L/1³/₄ pints.

Melt the butter in a saucepan and stir in the flour. Whisk in the reserved stock, and bring to the boil and make a sauce. Add the chicken and heat through. Blend the egg yolk and cream and whisk into the sauce.

Serves 6

LEEK AND POTATO SOUP

....

This is possibly my favourite winter soup. It is easy to make and tastes delicious. The big green leeks I was once given in Wales made soup that I shall always remember – the flavour was outstanding!

50g/2 oz butter
1 onion, chopped
450g/1 lb leeks, trimmed, washed and sliced
2 potatoes, chopped
1L/2 pints vegetable or chicken stock
1 tsp salt
pepper
2–3 tablespoons cream

Melt the butter in a large frying pan and sauté the onion and leeks until soft. Add the potatoes and toss in the butter. Cover and cook gently for a few minutes, until the potatoes are softening. Stir in the stock, salt and pepper. Cover and bring to the boil. Transfer to the simmering oven for an hour. Purée the soup, check the seasoning and serve in bowl with a little cream stirred in.

....
Serves 6
....

CELERY SOUP

....

This is a variation on the celery soup in *The Traditional Aga Cookery Book*. The potatoes act as a thickening agent. Grated cheese at the end will make this into a substantial meal.

50g/2 oz butter
1 onion, chopped
1 head celery, washed and sliced
450g/1 lb potatoes, peeled and sliced
1 L/1³/₄ pints chicken or vegetable stock
salt and pepper
150ml/¹/₄ pint cream

Heat the butter in a flameproof casserole and sauté the onion, celery and potatoes. Cook gently until softening but not browning. Add the stock and a seasoning of salt and pepper. Cover, bring to the boil and transfer to the simmering oven for about 1 hour.

Purée the soup. Check the seasoning and pour in the cream just before serving.

Serves 4–6
....

FRENCH ONION SOUP

....

The long, slow cooking of the onions to caramelise them without burning is effortlesssly achieved in the simmering oven.

25g/1 oz butter
450g/1lb onions, sliced
1.2L/2 pints light stock
¹/₂ tsp salt
25g/1 oz flour mixed with 150ml/1/4 pint water
4-6 slices French bread
50g/2 oz Gruyère cheese

Melt the butter in a large saucepan and stir in the onions. Cover and when the onions are piping hot, transfer to the simmering oven for an hour. Add the stock and salt, and bring back to the boil. Return to the simmering oven for a further hour. Stir in the flour mixture and boil for 2–3 minutes.

Place the French bread on a baking sheet, sprinkle on the grated Gruyère and toast for a few minutes at the top of the roasting oven. Place one piece in each soup dish and pour round the soup.

Serves 4–6
....

CRÉCY SOUP

This soup is named after the small town in France named Crécy that produces good root vegetables, especially carrots. 150ml/¹/₄ pint of orange juice can be stirred in at the end if you like carrot and orange soup.

75g/3 oz butter
225g/8 oz carrots, sliced
1 onion, sliced
salt and pepper
25g/1 oz white rice
1 sprig thyme
600ml/1 pint light stock

Melt the butter in a saucepan and sauté the carrots and onion. Season with salt and pepper, and cover. Allow the vegetables to sweat over a gentle heat for a few minutes. Add the rice, thyme and stock. Bring to the boil, transfer to the simmering oven for 1 hour. Remove the thyme and purée the soup. Check the seasoning and serve.

Serves 4

MINESTRONE

There are many variations on this recipe, largely depending upon the vegetables in season. Tiny pasta shapes can be added at the end of cooking, which particularly appeal to children.

100g/4 oz dried white cannellini beans or kidney beans,
soaked overnight
2 tbsp olive oil
1 large onion, finely chopped
2 carrots, finely diced
2 celery stalks, sliced
2 cloves garlic, crushed
2L/3 ¹/₂ pints chicken or vegetable stock
bouquet garni
¹/₂ small cabbage, finely shredded
2 courgettes, chopped
50g/2 oz mini pasta shapes
freshly grated Parmesan cheese, to serve

Rinse and drain the soaked beans. Heat the oil in a large flameproof casserole and sauté the onion, carrot, celery and garlic until softening but not colouring. Add the beans, the stock and bouquet garni. Cover and bring to the boil. Transfer to the simmering oven for 1¹/₂–2 hours.

Add the cabbage, courgettes and pasta shapes. Bring to the boil and return to the simmering oven for about 20 minutes. Check the seasoning. Serve with a little cheese on top.

Serves 8

LENTIL SOUP

....

This is a good soup to make if you have cooked a piece of ham, as the cooking liquid gives lentil soup a delicious flavour. Some crispy bacon can be served as a garnish if liked.

25g/1 oz butter
100g/4 oz lentils
2 carrots, diced
2 onions, chopped
1L/1³/₄ pints stock
salt and pepper

Heat the butter in a flameproof casserole and toss in the lentils. Add the carrots and onions, and sauté until the vegetables are softening.

Add the stock, bring to the boil, cover and transfer to the simmering oven for 1¹/₂–2 hours. Remove from the oven and purée the soup if liked. Check the seasoning and serve.

Serves 4–6
....

YELLOW SPLIT PEA SOUP

This is a substantial soup full of flavour from the ham. The peas used are not the green frozen variety!

275g/10 oz yellow split peas, soaked overnight
1 onion, finely sliced
2 celery stalks, chopped
piece of ham shank, soaked in water, about 450g/1 lb in weight
sprig of thyme
salt and pepper
chopped parsley, to garnish

Rinse the split peas well and place in a large saucepan. Add the onion, celery, ham and thyme. Cover with 1.5L/2³/₄ water. Cover, bring to the boil and after 1–2 minutes transfer to the simmering oven for 2–3 hours, until the peas and ham are tender. Remove the ham and purée the split peas. Check the seasoning. Serve with pieces of ham in each bowl and garnish with chopped parsley.

Serves 4–6

ADUKI BEAN SOUP

Aduki beans are like small kidney beans. This recipe is adaptable to any dried pulses you may have in the store cupboard. Larger beans make take a little more time to cook.

2 tbsp vegetable oil
1 onion, chopped
1 celery stalk, chopped
1 carrot, diced
1 clove garlic, crushed
100g/4 oz aduki beans, soaked overnight
4 tomatoes, peeled and chopped
1 tbsp tomato purée
bouquet garni
1 L/1³/₄ pints water or light stock
salt and pepper
chopped parsley, to garnish

Heat the oil in a flameproof casserole and sauté the onion, celery, carrot and garlic until soft but not brown. Add the drained beans, tomatoes, tomato purée, bouquet garni and the water or stock. Cover and bring to the boil. Transfer to the simmering oven for 2 hours. Check the seasoning. Sprinkle with chopped parsley just before serving.

Serves 4–6

PÂTÉS

Pâtés are easy to make, especially with the aid of a food processor. However, if you like a coarse pâté, take care not to over-process the mixture. Alternatively, you can use a mincer.

Pâtés can be cooked with a bain-marie in the roasting oven, alternatively cook for longer in the simmering oven after 30 minutes in the roasting oven. Always use the cold shelf in the roasting oven. If you think the pâté is crisping too much on the top, cover with a sheet of foil.

THRIFTY PÂTÉ

A good family pâté, economical and easy to make.

650g/1¹/₂lb lean belly pork, roughly chopped
225g/8 oz pig's liver
100g/4 oz streaky bacon, rind removed
1 clove garlic, crushed
1 onion, chopped
1 tsp salt
pepper
¹/₄ tsp ground coriander

Place all the ingredients in a food processor and process to make a smooth pâté. Press into a 1kg/2 lb 4oz loaf tin. Place in the small roasting tin and pour boiling water round the loaf tin. Cover the loaf tin with a sheet of foil. Hang on the bottom set of runners in the roasting oven, slide the cold shelf on the runner above and cook for 30 minutes. Transfer to the simmering oven for 2-3 hours, until the pâté has shrunk from the sides of the tin. Weigh down the pâté and chill. For the electric oven cook at 150°C for 1¹/₂-2 hours.

8–10 slices

FARMHOUSE PÂTÉ

A flavoursome pâté that should have a coarse texture.

100g/4 oz streaky bacon
225g/8 oz belly pork
225g/8 oz stewing veal
100g/4 oz pig's liver
salt and pepper
pinch powdered mace
2 tbsp white wine
1 tbsp brandy
2 cloves garlic, crushed

Remove the rind from the bacon. Reserve half the rashers and use these to line a 1kg/2 lb 4 oz loaf tin. Place the remaining ingredients in a processor and mince until all is chopped and blended, but not too fine. Press the mixture into the loaf tin. Stand the loaf tin in the small roasting tin and pour round hot water to come about halfway up the sides of the loaf tin.

Slide on to the bottom set of runners of the roasting oven, put the cold shelf on the runner above and cook for 1½ hours, or for 30 minutes and then transfer to the simmering oven for 2-3 hours. Alternatively cook in an electric oven at 150°C for 1½ hours. The pâté will have shrunk from the sides of the tin.
Chill the pâté and weigh down the top until completely cold.

8–10 slices

GAME PÂTÉ

A pâté to make in minutes using a food processor. This recipe uses only a small amount of game, but I find the meat from two pigeons gives an intensely flavoured, but not too rich pâté.

1 onion, chopped
25g/1 oz butter, melted
400g/14 oz sausage meat
½ tsp freshly grated nutmeg
2 tbsp brandy
salt and pepper
225g/8 oz game meat e.g. pigeon
1 egg

Put the onion, butter, sausage meat, nutmeg, brandy, salt and plenty of pepper into a food processor. Whizz round until all is mixed and the onion is chopped finely. Add the game and the egg, and whizz to just chop the meat and combine the egg.

Press into a 1.2L/2 pint oven-proof dish. Cover, and stand in the small roasting tin. Pour boiling water round the dish. Hang on the bottom set of runners of the roasting oven and slide the cold shelf on to the second set of runners from the bottom. Cook for 30 minutes and then transfer to the simmering oven for 2 hours. Remove and chill before serving.

Serves 6

COARSE LIVER TERRINE

This is a coarse loaf rather than a smooth pâté. The sausage meat keeps the mixture moist and makes this an economical dish.

450g/1 lb pigs or lamb's liver
25g/1 oz butter
2 onions, chopped
100g/4 oz bacon, rind removed
100g/4 oz fresh breadcrumbs
225g/8 oz sausage meat
2 tsp Worcestershire sauce
1 tbsp lemon juice
salt and pepper
2 eggs, beaten

Remove any tubes from the liver and then roughly chop. Melt the butter in a frying pan and cook the liver and onions until golden brown.

Transfer the contents of the pan to a food processor along with the bacon, breadcrumbs, sausage meat, Worcestershire sauce and lemon juice. Whizz to just chop, then add salt and pepper, and the eggs. Whizz once more. Press the mixture into a 1kg/2 lb 4 oz loaf tin.

Stand the loaf tin in the small roasting tin and pour water round to come about half-way up the sides of the loaf tin. Cover with a sheet of foil. Hang the tin on the bottom set of runners of the roasting oven, and slide the cold shelf on to the runner above. Cook for 30 minutes, then transfer to the simmering oven for 2 hours. If using an electric oven, cook at 180°C for 1 1/2 hours. The loaf can be served hot with a tomato sauce, or cold as a pâté.

Serves 8–10

H O U M M U S

....

This chick-pea spread can be eaten as a pâté. It is particularly nice with triangles of pitta bread and cold roast vegetables. My son Dominic likes it so much he had been known to eat it on hot cross buns !

225g/8 oz chick-peas, soaked overnight
salt
4 tbsp tahini/(sesame paste)
2 cloves garlic, crushed
4 tbsp lemon juice, or to taste
2 tbsp olive oil

Drain the chick-peas and put in a saucepan, cover with water and bring to the boil on the boiling plate. Cover and transfer to the simmering oven for 1^1/$_2$–2 hours, until the chick-peas are well cooked.

Drain the chick-peas, reserving some of the liquid. Transfer to a food processor with salt, the tahini, garlic, lemon juice and olive oil. Blend until smooth, adding some of the cooking liquid if necessary. Taste and add more lemon juice or salt as needed.

MAIN COURSE

MAIN COURSES

PAPRIKA BEEF CASSEROLE

This recipe has a hint of Eastern Europe – the use of the paprika, combined with the tomato paste makes a thick, tasty sauce. If you don't have cider then use red wine instead for the marinade.

4 tsp paprika
6 tsp tomato purée
300ml/ ¹/₂ pint cider
1 tsp salt
1kg/2 lb 4oz stewing beef, cut into large dice
2 tbsp vegetable oil
2 onions, sliced
3 carrots, thickly sliced

Mix together the paprika, tomato purée, cider and salt in a non-metallic bowl. Stir in the beef, coat well and cover. Leave to marinate for about 8 hours or overnight.

Heat the oil in a flameproof casserole and sauté the onion and carrots until softening. Stir in the beef and the marinade. Bring to the boil. Add a little water if necessary. Cover and transfer to the simmering oven. Cook for 4–5 hours or in an electric oven at 130°C. The finished dish should produce its own thick gravy.

Serves 6

P O T   R O A S T   B E E F   I N   R E D   W I N E

This is a delicious way to cook topside or silverside, which can be rather dry when plainly roasted. The vegetables give richness to the meat and make a wonderful sauce.

2 tbsp cooking oil
1kg/2.2 lb silverside or topside beef
2 carrots, cut into large dice
2 parsnips, cut into large dice
1 large onion, cut into quarters
2 cloves garlic, crushed
2 tbsp tomato purée
2 bay leaves
pinch sugar
salt and pepper
¹/₂ bottle red wine

Heat the oil in a flameproof casserole and brown the meat all over. Remove to a plate. Add the prepared vegetables to the casserole and sauté until just beginning to colour. Sir in the tomato purée, bay leaves, sugar, salt and pepper, and wine. Place the meat on top. Cover and slowly bring to the boil on the simmering plate. Simmer for 10 minutes and then transfer to the simmering oven for 3–4 hours or the electric oven at 150 °C for the same time.

To serve: the braising vegetables may be served as they are or puréed to make a sauce. Slice the meat into thick slices.

Serves 6

DAUBE DE BOEUF

....

This must be one of the easiest casserole recipes. I have adapted this from my much used *French Provincial Cooking* by Elizabeth David. A flameproof casserole dish with a tight fitting lid is best. This doesn't work so well in an electric oven, it is best simmering on a thread of heat on the hob, but of course it works brilliantly in the simmering oven.

> *175g/6 oz unsmoked streaky bacon, rinded and cubed*
> *2 tbsp olive oil*
> *2 onions, sliced*
> *2 carrots, sliced*
> *2 tomatoes, peeled and sliced*
> *1kg/2 lb 4oz braising or top rump beef*
> *bouquet garni*
> *2 cloves garlic, lightly crushed*
> *salt and pepper*
> *125ml/4 fl oz red wine*

Lay the bacon in the base of the casserole dish, along with the olive oil. Then layer in the onions and carrots and the tomatoes. Lay on the meat and bury the bouquet garni and garlic amongst the meat. Season with salt and pepper. Stand on the simmering plate and start warming through gently.

Pour the wine into a small saucepan and bring it to a fast boil. Set it alight. When the flames have died down pour the wine over the meat. Cover with a lid, make sure the casserole is thoroughly heated and then transfer to the simmering oven for 3-4 hours. This is often served with pasta that has been tossed with the fat from the top of the meat.

Serves 6

....

PROVENÇAL BEEF STEW

....

This is a simple beef casserole made a little different by the addition of black olives at the end of cooking. Olive oil used for the frying process will help give the Mediterranean flavour.

700g/1 ¹/₂ lb stewing beef
2 tbsp seasoned flour
4 tbsp olive oil
4 carrots, sliced
2 onions, chopped
2 cloves garlic, crushed
100g/4 oz mushrooms, sliced
300ml/¹/₂ pint red wine
150ml/¹/₄ pint beef stock
about 12 black olives
salt and pepper

Cut the meat into large cubes and toss in the seasoned flour. Heat the oil in a frying pan and brown the meat. Transfer to a casserole dish. Cook the carrots, onions and garlic in the hot pan until the onions are softening and only slightly coloured.

Add the mushrooms, the red wine and stock, and bring to the boil. Pour over the meat. Cover, bring to the boil and transfer to the simmering oven for 3–4 hours, or the electric oven at 150°C for 3 hours. Add the olives and check the seasoning before serving.

....
Serves 6
....

CLASSIC BEEF CASSEROLE

A simple beef casserole using store-cupboard ingredients and a cheaper cut of meat. The flavour will be good after the long, slow cooking. For variety, the mustard may be replaced with 2 tablespoons of chutney.

700g /1¹/₂ lb beef skirt
25g/1 oz seasoned flour
1 tbsp vegetable oil
25g 1 oz butter
1 large onion, chopped
3 carrots, thickly sliced
2 tsp mustard
450ml/³/₄ pint beef stock

Cut the meat into large cubes and toss in the seasoned flour. Heat the oil and butter in a large frying pan and brown the meat on all sides. Drain and place in a casserole dish.

In the heated pan, sauté the onion and carrots until the onion is just starting to colour and slightly soften. Add to the meat. Stir the mustard into the pan and scrape off any residue from the base of the pan before stirring in the stock. Stir well, bring to the boil and pour over the meat. Bring to the boil and transfer to the simmering oven for 4–5 hours, or the electric oven at 140°C. Thicken the gravy (see page 21) if liked before serving.

Serves 6

MEXICAN CHILLI CON CARNE

This recipe originated in Mexico as a way of using up stringy beef. I cook it and serve it in taco shells or with rice for a crowd of people. Soured cream and guacamole are delicious spooned on top.

2 tbsp vegetable oil
2 large onions, finely chopped
350g/12 oz minced beef
350g/12 oz minced pork
2 cloves garlic, crushed
2 tsp chilli powder
1 tbsp dried oregano
1 tbsp cumin seeds, lightly crushed
450g/1 lb tomatoes, peeled and seeded
1 tbsp red wine vinegar
1 tsp sugar
salt and pepper
300g/11 oz cooked red kidney beans, or a large can, drained

Heat the oil in a large flameproof casserole and sauté the onion until soft. Add the meats and stir over a high heat until broken up and browned. Add the garlic, chilli powder, oregano, cumin seeds and tomatoes, stir well and bring to the boil. Add the wine vinegar, sugar, and salt and pepper. Cover and transfer to the simmering oven for at least 1 hour.

Remove from the oven and skim any fat and then stir in the kidney beans. Return to the oven for a further half 30 minutes. Adjust seasoning and serve.

Serves 6

STEAK AND KIDNEY PUDDING

An old British pudding traditionally served with a starched napkin tied over the top. The gentle cooking in the simmering oven lends itself to cooking this dish.

700g/1 ¹/₂lb stewing beef, cubed
225g/8 oz ox or lamb kidney, cored and cubed
25g/1 oz seasoned flour
1 large onion, chopped
1 tbsp chopped parsley
salt and pepper
about 150ml/¹/₄ pint beef stock

SUET PASTRY:

450g/1lb self-raising flour
225g/8 oz shredded suet
pinch of salt

To make the pastry, sift the flour, mix with the suet and salt, and enough water to bind. Toss the beef and kidneys in the seasoned flour. Line a 1.7L/3 pint pudding basin with three-quarters of the suet pastry. Fill the basin with alternate layers of steak, kidney and onions. Sprinkle each layer with parsley and a little salt and pepper. Add enough stock to just cover the meat. Use the remaining pastry to make a lid for the pudding. Seal the lid firmly. Cover with a layer of pleated greaseproof paper followed by foil or a pudding cloth.

Stand the basin in a saucepan deep enough to take the pudding with a lid on. Pour sufficient boiling water into the pan to come halfway up the sides of the basin. Cover and bring to the boil and simmer for 30 minutes on the simmering plate before transfering to the simmering oven for 6 hours.

Serves 6

STEAK AND KIDNEY PIE

The pie can be topped with shortcrust or puff pastry, but the puff pastry looks most spectacular when served. There are many variations on this recipe — mushrooms can be added, Worcestershire sauce used for flavouring, plain stock and no tomato purée used. Some regions pour in cream just before serving!

675g/1 lb 8oz stewing steak, cubed
225g/8 oz kidneys, cored and chopped
1 tbsp seasoned flour
2 tbsp vegetable oil
1 large onion, chopped
300ml/¹/₂ pint beef stock
150ml/¹/₄ pint red wine
1 tbsp tomato purée
1 tbsp chopped parsley
salt and pepper
225g/8 oz puff pastry
a little beaten egg, to glaze

Toss the steak and kidney in the seasoned flour. Heat the oil in a pan and brown the meat well. Transfer to a casserole dish. Add the onion to the hot fat and fry for a minute or two. Stir the stock, red wine, tomato purée, parsley, salt, pepper and onion into the meat. Bring to the boil, cover and transfer to the simmering oven for 4–5 hours, or the electric oven at 150°C for 4 hours.

Place the meat mixture in a pie dish and roll out the pastry to fit. Place a ceramic pie funnel in the middle of the pie dish and dampen the edges of the dish. Place a strip of pastry round the edge of the dish. Dampen then cover the pie with the pastry. Make a hole in the centre and decorate the edges. Brush with beaten egg. Place in the roasting oven on the third set of runners from the top, or the electric oven at 210°C for 25–30 minutes until the pastry is puffy and golden brown.

Serves 6

CARBONNADE OF BEEF

A rich casserole of beef cooked slowly and topped off with slices of crisp mustard-coated French bread. Add the bread at the last moment otherwise the base of the bread will be soggy!

700g/1lb 8 oz braising steak, sliced
1 tbsp seasoned flour
1 tbsp vegetable oil
50g/2 oz butter
50g/2 oz streaky bacon, rinded and diced
3 large onions, sliced
300 ml/^{1}/$_2$ pint brown ale
150 ml/^{1}/$_4$ pint beef stock
5 tsp mustard
bouquet garni
salt and pepper
6 thick slices French bread

Toss the beef in the flour, Heat the oil and butter in a frying pan and brown the bacon. Transfer to a casserole dish.

Sauté the onions in the hot fat until softening but not browning. Drain and transfer to the casserole dish. Brown the meat on all sides and then add to the bacon and onions in the casserole. Sprinkle any remaining flour into the frying pan and stir well. Gradually whisk in the brown ale, the stock and one teaspoon of the mustard. Bring to the boil and pour over the meat in the casserole. Add the bouquet garni, cover and bring to the boil. Transfer to the simmering oven for 2–2 ^{1}/$_2$ hours, or the electric oven at 170°C.

Remove bouquet garni, and check the seasoning. Spread one side of each piece of bread with the remaining mustard and place on top of meat, mustard side uppermost. Place the casserole, without the lid, on the shelf on the bottom set of runners of the roasting oven, for 15 minutes, until the bread is crisp.

Serves 6

BRAISED OXTAIL CASSEROLE

This is a classic winter dish that has a full flavour. Cooking in the simmering oven brings out all the flavours. Oxtail can be a little fatty, so if this is made the day before serving, the fat can be skimmed off the top.

1 whole oxtail, cut into pieces
salt and pepper
2 tbsp vegetable oil
1 tbsp flour
25g/1 oz butter
1 large onion, finely chopped
2 large carrots, finely diced
4 celery stalks, finely sliced
300ml/½ pint red wine
1 tbsp tomato paste
1 bouquet garnis
600ml/1 pint beef stock

Season the oxtail with salt and pepper. Heat the oil in a frying pan and brown the oxtail pieces all over. Remove and place in a casserole dish. Sprinkle the flour over the oxtail pieces.

Wipe out the frying pan and melt the butter in it. Sauté the onion, carrots and celery until starting to soften. Pour on the wine, bubble for a minute and then stir in the tomato paste. Add the bouquet garni to the meat and pour on the wine and vegetable mixture. Add the stock, cover, bring to the boil and then place in the simmering oven, or the electric oven at 150°C, for 4–5 hours, until the meat is tender and coming off the bone. The sauce may be skimmed and strained before serving.

Serves 4

PRESSED SALT BEEF

....

Salt beef can be bought from a traditional butcher. When cooked and pressed it slices thinly for sandwiches and salads. Keep it wrapped in greaseproof paper in the fridge.

2kg/4 lb 8 oz salted brisket of beef
1 onion, stuck with cloves
1 large carrot, thickly sliced
1 stick celery
1 bouquet garni
12 peppercorns

Soak the meat in cold water for 1 hour then drain. Place the meat in a saucepan or flameproof casserole along with the remaining ingredients. Just cover with fresh water. Bring to the boil, then transfer to the simmering oven for 4–5 hours.

Remove the meat, stand on a plate and press under a heavy weight for several hours until cold and set. Serve thinly sliced.

Serves 12
....

BRAISED AND SPICED TOPSIDE OF BEEF

Topside of beef can be a little on the dry side, so braising is a good, moist way to cook it. This is an easy way to cook a joint of beef for a large number of people. It is delicious served cold in thin slices. The cooking onions can be served with the hot meat or made into a tasty soup if the meat is served cold.

2kg/4 lb 8oz topside, boned and rolled
2 tsp salt
1 tsp ground allspice
3 tsp ground ginger
450ml/³/₄ pint cider
1 cinnamon stick
6 cloves
1 tbsp black peppercorns
2 blades mace
2 tbsp olive oil
2 onions, sliced
1 large carrot, sliced

Wipe the beef and rub with the salt, allspice and ginger. Put the cider, cinnamon stick, cloves, peppercorns and mace into a saucepan and bring to the boil. Put the meat in a non-metallic dish and pour over the cider mixture. Allow to cool and then marinade in a cool place for 48 hours, turning periodically. Heat the oil in a large frying pan. Pat the meat dry and brown all over in the hot pan. Transfer to a casserole dish, or the small roasting tin. Add the vegetables to the hot pan and sauté until just softening. Add to the meat. Pour the marinade into the hot frying pan and bring to the boil. Pour over the meat. Hang the tin on the bottom set of runners of the roasting oven for 30–40 minutes, then transfer to the simmering oven for 3–4 hours, depending upon the thickness of the beef joint and how rare you like the meat. If using an electric oven start at 190°C for the first half hour then turn down to 170°C.

Serves 8-10

BOLOGNESE SAUCE

....

For a rich, fully-flavoured sauce cook this slowly in the simmering oven. This sauce freezes well, so I usually make a large quantity at a time and use to make lasagnes as well as spaghettis. This makes enough lasagne for 6.

2 tbsp olive oil
450g/1 lb lean minced beef
2–3 rashers bacon, rinded and chopped
1 onion, finely chopped
1 carrot, finely chopped
1 small celery stalk, finely diced
1 clove garlic, crushed
50g/2 oz mushrooms, finely diced
400g/14 oz can chopped tomatoes
1 tbsp tomato purée
1 bay leaf
150ml/¹/₄ pint red wine
pinch dried oregano
salt and pepper

Heat the oil in a flameproof casserole and fry the minced beef and bacon until browned. Drain and reserve. Sauté the onion, carrot and celery until softening. Add the garlic and the mushrooms, and cook for 1 or 2 more minutes.

Return the meat to the pan, add the tomatoes, tomato purée, bay leaf, red wine, oregano, and salt and pepper. Stir well, bring to the boil, cover and transfer to the simmering oven for 1–2 hours.

Serves 6
....

....

BEEF LASAGNE

Lasagne remains a very popular dish. It is good when catering for a crowd, but can be time consuming to make. Cook the sauce slowly for a good rich flavour.

2 tbsp olive oil
2 onions, finely chopped
2 cloves garlic, crushed
1kg/2 lb 4 oz good quality minced beef
225g/8 oz mushrooms, finely chopped
400g/14 oz can chopped tomatoes
3 tbsp tomato purée
150ml/¼ pint red wine
1 tbsp chopped fresh basil, or ½ tsp dried oregano
2 bay leaves
salt and pepper
60ml/1 pint milk
50g/2 oz flour
50g/2 oz butter
225g/8 oz ready-to-use lasagne
75g/3 oz grated Gruyère cheese

In a flameproof casserole heat the olive oil and sauté the onion. When soft but not coloured, add the crushed garlic and the minced beef. Stir to break up the meat, and fry until brown. Add the mushrooms and fry for 2–3 minutes, then add the tomatoes, tomato purée, red wine, herbs, bay leaves, and a seasoning of salt and pepper. Cover, and bring to the boil, then transfer to the simmering oven for 1–2 hours. Butter an oblong oven-proof dish. Put the milk, flour, butter and salt and pepper into a saucepan and whisk over a medium heat until smooth. Spoon a little sauce into the base of the buttered dish. Lay on a layer of lasagne sheets and then a layer of meat sauce. Continue layering, finishing with lasagne and a topping of the sauce. Sprinkle on the grated cheese. Place the oven shelf on the bottom set of runners of the roasting oven and cook the lasagne for 40–50 minutes until golden brown, bubbling and the lasagne is cooked. For the electric oven cook at 170°C for the same time.

Serves 4-6

MAURITIAN CHICKEN CURRY

I made this recipe of Anton Mosimann's with squid for a cookery demonstration. Having some spices left I decided to use chicken for my family, and it works very well. It is not hot – add more chilli if you like it hot – but full of flavour.

1 tbsp coriander seeds
1 tsp cumin seeds
3 small shallots, chopped
2 cloves garlic
1 tsp finely chopped fresh ginger,
1 stalk lemon grass, chopped
3 fresh red chillies, seeded
2 tsp curry powder
1 tsp salt
2 tbsp vegetable oil
4 chicken portions, skinned
4 tomatoes, peeled, seeded and chopped
200ml/7 fl oz canned coconut milk
200ml/7 fl oz chicken stock
pepper

Dry-fry the coriander and cumin seeds in a frying pan. Place in a food processor or blender along with the shallots, garlic, ginger, lemon grass, chillies, curry powder and salt. Blend together to make a paste. Heat the vegetable oil in a flameproof casserole and brown the chicken. Remove and set aside. Sauté the curry paste in the hot casserole for about 5 minutes, stirring. Add the tomatoes, milk, stock and pepper, and bring to the boil.

Add the reserved chicken, cover and bring back to the boil, then cook in the simmering oven for 2–3 hours. For an electric cooker simmer over a low heat on the hob for 1–2 hours. Check the seasoning and serve.

Serves 4

HANNA'S CHICKEN WITH PEPPERS

This dish makes the most of those glorious looking red and green peppers. This is a great summer dish served with crisp salad and crusty bread. We have even eaten it cold as a salad, with the vegetables tossed in olive oil. The dish is named after my daughter who loves peppers and mushrooms.

1 tbsp olive oil
6 chicken portions
1 onion, sliced
1 clove garlic, crushed
1 large red pepper, seeded and cut into thick slices
1 large green pepper, seeded and cut into thick slices
175g/6 oz mushrooms, sliced
225g/8 oz tomatoes, skinned and sliced
150ml/¹/₄ pint white wine
1 tbsp tomato purée
salt and pepper
sprig fresh thyme

Heat the oil in a flameproof casserole and brown the chicken portions well. Drain and set aside.

Sauté the onion, garlic and peppers until softening, then add the mushrooms, tomatoes, wine, tomato purée, and salt and pepper. Add the thyme and push the chicken portions well into the vegetable mix. Cover and bring to the boil. Place in the simmering oven for 1¹/₂–2 hours or the electric oven at 180°C for 1¹/₂ hours.

Serves 6

CHICKEN AND DRIED FRUIT TAJINE

A tajine is a deep earthenware pot from the Middle East that gives its name to a stew – in this case chicken and dried fruits. Couscous is a very good accompaniment.

1 large chicken, jointed, or 6 chicken portions
1 lemon, halved
salt and pepper
2 onions, finely chopped
1 clove garlic, finely chopped
¹/₂ tsp ground cumin
¹/₂ tsp powdered saffron or pinch saffron strands
2 tbsp olive oil
1 cinnamon stick
1 strip lemon peel
300ml/¹/₂ pint chicken stock
225g/8 oz dried fruit, such as prunes, apricots and dates,
soaked, stoned and halved
3 tbsp clear honey
1 tbsp chopped fresh coriander
2 tbsp flaked almonds, sautéd in butter until pale gold

Rub the chicken all over with the lemon halves. Season with salt and pepper, and place in a dish. Mix together the onions, garlic, cumin, saffron and olive oil, and pour over the chicken. Mix well and leave to marinate, for at least an hour.

Skim the oil from the marinade into a frying pan and heat. Fry the chicken pieces, onion and garlic until golden brown. Drain and place in a casserole dish.

Add the cinnamon, lemon peel and stock to the casserole. Cover and bring to the boil, then place in the simmering oven for 1¹/₂ hours, until tender. If using an electric oven set the temperature to 160°C. Remove the chicken and place on a plate in the simmering oven to keep warm.

Add the dried fruits and honey to the casserole, bring to the boil, then transfer to the roasting oven for 15 minutes. Strain out the fruits and add to the chicken. Boil the remaining liquid over a high heat to reduce to a coating consistency. Return the chicken and fruit to the sauce to bubble through. Garnish with the coriander and almonds.

Serves 6

COQ AU VIN

Coq au Vin must be one of the most popular ways of cooking a chicken casserole. The combination of flavours works really well. The flavour of this dish really benefits from long, slow cooking.

2 tbsp olive oil
1 large chicken, jointed, or 6–8 chicken portions
1 onion, finely chopped
2 cloves garlic, crushed
100g/4 oz streaky bacon, rinded and chopped
150ml/¼ pint chicken stock
12 shallots, peeled
450ml/¾ pint red wine
salt and pepper
1 tsp dried tarragon
2 bay leaves
100g/4 oz button mushrooms
1 tbsp cornflour

Heat the oil in a large frying pan and brown the chicken joints. Drain and place in a large casserole dish. Add the onion and bacon to the pan and fry until the onion has softened, adding the garlic for the last minute. Drain and transfer to the casserole dish.

Add the wine to the pan and bring to the boil, then add the stock, salt and pepper, and tarragon. Bring to the boil and pour over the chicken.

Bury the shallot and bay leaves in the casserole. Cover and transfer to the simmering oven, or the electric oven at 160°C, for 1 ½ hours.

Stir in the mushrooms and return to the oven for a further 30 minutes. Blend the cornflour with water to make a smooth paste and stir into the casserole juices. Return to the oven for a further 15 minutes, until the sauce is thickened.

Serves 6–8

PEANUT CHICKEN CASSEROLE

The peanut butter makes a rich, moist sauce for the chicken and the whole peanuts add a delicious crunch.

6 chicken joints
2 tbsp seasoned flour
3 tbsp olive oil
1 onion, chopped
125ml/¹/₄ pint chicken stock
300ml/¹/₂ pint milk
2 tbsp smooth peanut butter
salt and pepper
3 tbsp single cream
50–75g/2–3 oz salted peanuts, roughly chopped

Coat the chicken portions with the seasoned flour. Heat the oil in a frying pan and cook the onion until soft. Drain and place in a casserole dish. Add the chicken to the hot oil and brown all over. Move to the casserole dish.

Add the stock to the pan along with the milk and peanut butter, bring to the boil, scraping all the residue from the base of the pan. Pour over the chicken. Season with salt and pepper. Cover the casserole and bring to the boil. Transfer to the simmering oven for 1–1¹/₂ hours. Cook in an electric oven at 150°C for the same time. Stir in the cream and check the seasoning. Sprinkle over the peanuts.

Serves 6

CHICKEN IN A POT

Choose a casserole dish that is large enough to hold your chicken whole with some room for the vegetables. If you want to use a larger chicken, increase the amount of vegetables to go with it.

1.5kg/3 lb chicken
1 tbsp vegetable oil
4 celery stalks, cut into thirds
1 leek, cut into thick rings
4 carrots, peeled and thickly sliced
2 onions, peeled and quartered
100g/4 oz button mushrooms
1 bouquet garni
300ml/¹/₂ pint chicken stock
salt and pepper

Heat the oil in a frying pan and brown the chicken all over – especially the breasts. Transfer to a plate.

Sauté the celery, leek, carrots and onion in the hot fat for 2–3 minutes, then add the mushrooms. When the vegetables are starting to soften, transfer them to a casserole dish. Add the bouquet garni and place the chicken on top. Pour over the stock and season with salt and pepper. Bring the casserole to a gentle boil and then transfer to the simmering oven for 4 hours. The chicken should be cooked but the vegetables should still have some 'bite' left. If using the electric oven cook for 3 hours at 160°C.

Serves 4

CHICKEN IN SHERRY SAUCE

A variation on chicken in wine! This is very simple to make and a useful way to use up the end of a bottle of sherry!

4 chicken portions
rind and juice of 1 lemon
150ml/¹/₄ pint sweet sherry
150ml/¹/₄ pint light chicken stock
50g/2 oz sultanas
¹/₂ tsp dried ginger
salt and pepper
1 tsp cornflour blended with water to thicken

Place the chicken in a non-metallic dish and add the rind and juice of the lemon, the sherry and stock, the sultanas and ginger, and a seasoning of salt and pepper. Leave to marinade somewhere cool for at least 1 hour.

Place the chicken and marinading ingredients in a flameproof casserole. Cover and bring to the boil. Transfer to the simmering oven for 1¹/₂–2 hours, or at 180°C for 1¹/₂ hours in the electric oven. Thicken the sauce with the cornflour (see page 21) before serving.

Serves 4

CHICKEN IN COCONUT

The coconut gives this chicken a delicious creamy flavour, but also a grainy texture. If you like hot curries add more fresh chilli or use dried chillies instead.

4 tbsp vegetable oil
50g/2 oz desiccated coconut, soaked in a little water
3 fresh red chillies, seeded and chopped
2 tsp coriander seeds
1 cinnamon stick
1 tsp cumin seeds
8 black peppercorns
4 cloves
1/2 tsp ground turmeric
400ml/14 oz can coconut milk
5 cloves garlic, chopped
1 cube of fresh ginger about 2.5cm/1 inch square, chopped
2 onions, chopped
1kg/2 lb 4 oz chicken joints
salt

Heat about 1 tablespoon of oil in a frying pan. Drain the soaked coconut and fry in the oil. Drain and reserve. To the hot pan add the chillies, coriander, cinnamon, cumin seed, peppercorns, cloves, and turmeric. Stir for 1–2 minutes, adding more oil if necessary.

Put this spice mixture into a food processor or blender with half the coconut milk, the garlic, ginger and half the onions, Blend to make a smooth paste.

Heat 3 tablespoons of oil in a flameproof casserole and sauté the remaining onions until soft. Add the spice mixture, sauté and then stir in the chicken. Add salt to taste and more coconut milk if necessary, to make a sauce. Cover, bring to the boil and transfer to the simmering oven for 3–4 hours or to the electric oven at 160°C for 3 hours.

Serves 5-6

BASQUE CHICKEN

This is a perfect casserole for my daughter who loves red peppers and olives. There are times of the year when red peppers become ridiculously expensive – at that time substitute green peppers or canned ones.

6 chicken portions
1 tbsp seasoned flour
1 tbsp olive oil
25g/1 oz butter
2 large onions, sliced
2 red peppers, seeded and sliced
100g/4 oz green olives
salt and pepper
225g/8 oz tomatoes, peeled and roughly chopped
300ml/¹/₂ pint chicken stock

Toss the chicken in the seasoned flour. Heat the oil and butter in a frying pan, and brown the chicken portions. Remove and place in a shallow casserole dish.

Add the onions, peppers and tomatoes to the frying pan and cook for about 10 minutes until softening. Season with salt and pepper Add the olives and pour over the chicken. Add enough stock to cover the chicken by three-quarters. Cover and bring to the boil. Transfer to the simmering oven for 1¹/₂–2 hours until the chicken is tender. Cook in an electric oven at 150°C. Thicken the sauce (see page 21) if necessary.

Serves 6

CHICKEN AND MUSHROOM LASAGNE

Most people I know love lasagne. This is a variation using chicken instead of the usual beef. The finished dish can be frozen before the final cooking stage. Thaw thoroughly before finally cooking.

1.3kg/3 lb oven-ready chicken
300ml/¹/₂ pint white wine
1 onion
trimmings from 1 leek
celery stalk
bay leaf
6 peppercorns
100g/4 oz butter
1 clove garlic, crushed
450g/1 lb mushrooms, trimmed and sliced
100g/4 oz plain flour
225g/8 oz Gruyère cheese, grated
300ml/¹/₂ pint single cream
3 tbsp pinenuts, (optional)
225g 8 oz ready-to-use lasagne
salt and pepper

Place the chicken in a large casserole. Add the wine, onion, leek trimmings, celery, bay leaf and peppercorns. Add enough water to come halfway up the chicken. Season with salt and pepper. Cover, bring to the boil and transfer to the simmering oven for 2¹/₂ hours until tender. Leave to cool a little.

Cut the chicken into bite-sized pieces, discarding the skin and bone. Strain the cooking liquor – you will need 1L/1³/₄ pints. If necessary reduce by rapid boiling to the amount required.

Melt the butter in a saucepan and sauté the mushrooms and garlic for about 10 minutes until softened. Drain from the butter and set aside. Add the flour to the melted butter and whisk in the reserved cooking liquor. Bring to the boil. Off the heat stir in the single cream and half the Gruyère cheese.

Butter a shallow oven-proof dish well and pour a little sauce into the bottom. Lay on a layer of pasta followed by half the chicken and mushrooms. Add a little more sauce and then continue as before. Finish with a layer of lasagne. Pour on any remaining sauce and sprinkle over the remaining Gruyère and the pinenuts, if using. Place the shelf on the bottom set of runners of the roasting oven and slide in the prepared lasagne. Bake for 45–60 minutes until golden brown and cooked. If using an electric oven cook at 200°C.

Serves 6

SWEET AND SOUR BARBECUED CHICKEN

This is a simple casserole dish that has a sweet–savoury taste. The chicken is tenderised by the pineapple marinade as well as gaining flavour.

825g/1 lb 13 oz can pineapple pieces, drained
bunch spring onions, trimmed and chopped
125ml/4 fl oz tomato ketchup
50ml/2 fl oz maple syrup
2 tbsp vinegar
juice ¹/₂ lemon
2 cloves garlic, crushed
salt and pepper
6 chicken quarters
3 tbsp vegetable oil

In a non-metallic bowl combine the pineapple, onions, tomato ketchup, maple syrup, vinegar, lemon juice, garlic, and salt and pepper. Mix well, then add the chicken, turning to coat well. Cover and leave to marinade in the fridge for 4–5 hours or overnight.

Scrape the marinade off the chicken. Heat the oil in a large frying pan, brown the chicken well and place in a casserole dish. Pour over the marinade, cover and bring to the boil. Transfer to the simmering oven, or the electric oven at 160°C, for 1 ¹/₂ hours, until the chicken is tender.

Serves 6

BRAISED CHICKEN AND CHICORY

....

Chicory is a much under-used vegetable. It is particularly nice braised and goes well with the chicken. The crème fraîche makes a creamy sauce.

25g/1 oz butter
2 tbsp oil
12 chicken thighs
3 heads chicory
3 teaspoons brown sugar
salt and pepper
6 shallots, finely chopped
juice 1 ¹/₂ lemons
200ml/8 fl oz dry white wine
250ml/9 fl oz crème fraîche
chopped parsley, to garnish

Heat the butter and oil in a frying pan and brown the chicken thighs. Drain and put in a casserole. Split the chicory heads lengthways and brown in the hot pan. Toss with the sugar and allow to caramelise a little. Add to the chicken and season with salt and pepper.

Sauté the shallots in the frying pan and when softened add the lemon juice and wine. Boil for 1-2 minutes and then whisk in the crème fraîche. Pour over the chicken, cover the casserole and gently bring to the boil on the simmering plate.

Transfer to the simmering oven and cook for 1–1¹/₂ hours until the chicken is tender. For an electric oven cook at 150°C for 1–1¹/₂ hours. Check the seasoning, garnish with parsley and serve.

....
Serves 6
....

DUCK BREASTS IN WHITE WINE

Many people think duck is a fatty meat. This method removes the fat, keeps the meat moist but still retains the delicious flavour of duck.

4 duck breasts
1 onion, sliced
1 large carrot sliced
1 celery stalk, sliced
300ml/¹/₂ pint dry white wine
salt and pepper
mashed potatoes, to serve

Remove the skin and attached layer of fat from the duck breasts. Place some of the skin fat in a flameproof casserole and heat until 2–3 tablespoons of fat run. Remove the skin and brown the meat on all sides. Remove from the pan.

Now sauté the vegetables in the hot fat until softening. Return the duck to the pan and pour in the wine. Bring to a fast boil, then season with salt and pepper.

Cover and place in the simmering oven, or electric oven at 150°C, for 2–3 hours. Serve with lots of mashed potatoes to soak up the juices.

Serves 4

RABBIT IN THE DAIRY

This old English recipe has such a wonderful name that I couldn't resist trying it! This is a mild flavoured recipe, suitable for young or farmed rabbit. As there is very little colour in the finished dish, serve some brightly coloured fresh vegetables with it.

2 rabbits, jointed, or enough portions for 8
6 rashers bacon, rinded and diced
2 large onions, finely chopped
salt and pepper
a blade of mace or a pinch of ground mace
1.2L/2 pints milk
25g/1 oz cornflour

Wash and dry the rabbit, and place in a casserole dish. Add the bacon, onions, salt, pepper and mace. Pour over the milk, cover and bring to the boil. Transfer to the simmering oven and cook for 3 hours. If using an electric oven cook at 180°C for 2 hours.

Remove the rabbit joints and keep warm. Blend the cornflour with a little milk or water and stir into the cooking liquid. Boil, stirring to thicken the sauce. Adjust the seasoning, pour over the rabbit and serve.

Serves 6–8

RABBIT WITH DIJON MUSTARD

Rabbit makes very good casserole meat and goes particularly well with mustard. If rabbit is not available, chicken may be substituted. Wild rabbit has much more flavour than farmed rabbit, if you have the choice.

1 tbsp olive oil
25g/1 oz butter
100g/1 lb rabbit joints
2 small onions, finely chopped
225g/8 oz mushrooms, sliced
2 tbsp brandy
150ml/¹/₄ pint chicken stock
150ml/¹/₄ pint double cream
4–6 tbsp Dijon mustard
salt and pepper
chopped parsley, to garnish

Heat the oil and butter in a frying pan and brown the rabbit pieces all over. Drain and transfer to a plate.

Soften the onions and mushrooms in the hot pan, then pour on the brandy, warm through and ignite. When the flames have died down pour in the chicken stock and whisk in the double cream. Simmer gently while you smear the mustard over the rabbit portions. Place these in a casserole dish pour over the sauce and season. Simmer gently, cover and transfer to the simmering oven for 1–1¹/₂ hours. Check the seasoning and serve sprinkled with chopped parsley. Cook in an electric oven for 1–1¹/₂ hours at 160°C.

Serves 4

HARE STEW WITH WHISKY

Jugged hare is a classic English dish, but few people have access to the necessary fresh hare and its blood. So this recipe is a modern adaptation. If hare is not available use rabbit, stewing venison and older game birds.

1 hare, jointed
25g/1 oz flour, seasoned with salt and paprika
50g/2 oz butter
100g/4 oz bacon, each rasher quartered
2 large onions, finely chopped
4 celery stalks, chopped
2 sprigs each thyme and mint
2 tsp Worcestershire sauce
150ml ¼ pint whisky
450ml/¾ pint stock, either from hare trimmings
or good beef stock

Coat the joints of hare with the seasoned flour. In a frying pan, heat the butter and bacon, and when the fat has run from the bacon add the hare joints. Fry until browned all over, then transfer the hare and bacon to a casserole dish.

Fry the onions until softened and then add the celery. Cook until the celery is softened and the onion is golden brown. Stir in the whiskey, stock and Worcestershire sauce. Bring to the boil and pour over the hare. Tuck in the fresh herbs, cover with a lid and bring back to the boil. Transfer to the simmering oven for about 4 hours. If using an electric oven cook at 170°C for 3 hours.

Serves 6–8

PIGEON WITH RAISINS

Pigeon needs long, slow cooking to tenderise it – unless you know it is a young pigeon, in which case it can be roasted. Most recipes these days remove the breast meat and use the remaining meat and bones to make a stock. This recipe uses the whole bird, one per person.

50g/2 oz butter
3 tbsp olive oil
4 pigeons
100g/4 oz raisins, soaked in warm water for 30 minutes
4 large onions, thinly sliced
¹/₂ tsp paprika
salt and pepper

Heat the butter and oil in a frying pan, and brown the pigeons well all over. Transfer to a casserole dish. Cook the onions in the hot fat until soft and golden brown. Season with salt, pepper and paprika, and add to the pigeons along with the drained raisins. Cover with a well fitting lid or a sheet of foil. Heat gently on the simmering plate for a few minutes before transferring to the simmering oven for about 3 hours. If using an electric oven cook at 150°C for the same time.

Serves 4

PHEASANT WITH MUSHROOMS

A traditional way to cook jointed pheasants. The length of cooking time will depend upon the age of the birds. A larger cock bird should serve four, or two hen birds should serve six.

1 tbsp oil
50g/2 oz butter
2 onions, sliced
3 carrots, sliced
1 pheasant, jointed
1 tbsp brandy
a bouquet garni
450ml/³/₄ pint red wine
salt and pepper
8 shallots, peeled
8 button mushrooms
2 tbsp double cream

Heat the oil and half the butter in a frying pan and sauté the onion and carrots until soft. Drain and place in a casserole dish. Brown the pheasant portions in the hot pan and when browned all over pour on the brandy. When the brandy is hot, ignite with a match. Allow the flames to die down then transfer the pheasant to a casserole dish.

Pour the wine into the frying pan and bring to the boil, scraping all the sediment from the base of the pan. Season and pour over the pheasant. Add the bouquet garni. Cover, bring to the boil and transfer to the simmering oven for 3–4 hours. If using an electric oven cook at 160°C for 2–3 hours. Towards the end of cooking time, heat the remaining butter in a frying pan and fry the shallots and mushrooms until lightly golden brown. Drain the gravy from the casserole into a saucepan and boil to reduce. The gravy may be thickened (see page 21) if liked. Stir in the shallots, mushrooms and cream. Bubble gently for 2-3 minutes. Taste and adjust the seasoning. Pour over the pheasant.

Serves 4–6

NORMANDY POT-ROAST PHEASANT

This is a recipe for older pheasants that are not suitable for roasting. The bird can take up to 5 hours to become really tender in the simmering oven, but the long, slow cooking will be rewarded with a wonderfully intense flavour.

1 pheasant
25g/1 oz seasoned flour
50g/2 oz butter
2 onions, chopped
2 celery stalks, chopped
2 apples, peeled and cored
150ml/¹/₄ pint stock
150ml/¹/₄ pint dry cider
bouquet garni
150ml/¹/₄ pint double cream
2 eating apples, cored, sliced and fried in butter, to garnish

Dust the pheasant with the flour. Melt the butter in a frying pan and brown the pheasant all over. Remove and put into a casserole dish. Fry the onion and celery in the remaining hot fat in the pan until softening, then add the apples.

Add any remaining flour to the frying pan and stir well. Gradually add the stock and the cider. Bring to the boil and pour over the pheasant. Add the bouquet garni, cover and return to the boil. Then transfer to the simmering oven for 4–5 hours, until tender. For an electric oven cook at 160°C for 3–4 hours.

When tender, strain off the sauce into a small saucepan. If necessary boil to reduce to a thick, glossy sauce. Stir in the cream and check the seasoning. Serve garnished with the fried apple slices.

Serves 4–6

VENISON AND BEEF CASSEROLE

Venison adds a richness to beef casserole and casseroling is a good method of cooking cheaper cuts for a special dish.

450g/1 lb stewing venison
450g/1 lb stewing beef
300ml/¹/₂ pint robust red wine
2 tbsp olive oil
bouquet garni
salt and pepper
2 onions, sliced
2 carrots, thickly sliced

Cut the venison and beef into large dice and place in a non-metallic dish. Pour on the red wine, olive oil and add the bouquet garni, seasoning with salt and pepper. Cover and leave in a cool place for 12 hours or overnight.

Skim some of the oil from the top of the marinade and heat in a flameproof casserole. Drain the meat from the marinade and brown in the hot oil. Drain and transfer to a plate. Toss the onion and carrot in the hot oil and brown lightly. Return the meat to the casserole and pour on the remaining marinade. Bring gently to the boil and simmer for 5 minutes before transferring to the simmering oven for 4 hours, or the electric oven at 150 °C for 4 hours. If liked thicken the gravy before serving (see page 21).

Serves 6

LAMB CASSOULET

Traditionally, Cassoulet is a bean and meat stew from the Languedoc region of France but different regions use different meats. This is a fairly straightforward recipe using simple ingredients readily available. Cheap stewing lamb on the bone will give flavour and will be sweet and tender to eat.

225g/8 oz dried haricot beans
225g/8 oz piece green streaky bacon
1 onion, stuck with 4 cloves
1 carrot, sliced
2 cloves garlic, peeled
bouquet garni
salt and pepper
1kg/2 lb 2 oz stewing lamb
6 meaty sausages
1 tbsp olive oil
400g/14 oz can chopped tomatoes
1 tbsp tomato purée
50g/2 oz fresh breadcrumbs
50g/2 oz butter, melted

Soak the beans overnight, drain and put in a large casserole. Cut the bacon into large dice and add to the beans with the onion, carrot, garlic and bouquet garni. Barely cover with water and bring to the boil on the boiling plate. Transfer to the simmering oven for 1 hour until the beans are just tender.

Season the meat and sausages. Heat the olive oil in a frying pan and brown the lamb and the sausages on all sides. Remove the casserole from the oven and stir in the tomatoes and tomato purée. Lay the lamb and sausages on top. Cover and bring back to the boil on the simmering plate. Return to the simmering oven or electric oven at 120°C, for 3–4 hours. Sprinkle the breadcrumbs over the meat, then pour over the melted butter. Return to the oven and cook, uncovered, for a further hour.

Serves 6

L A M B   G O U L A S H

....

A lamb and paprika stew topped off with plain yoghurt to make a creamy sauce. Serve with noodles or creamy mashed potatoes.

1kg/2 lb 4 oz middle neck of lamb
50g/2 oz butter
2 onions, sliced
150ml /¹/₄ pint red wine
4 tsp paprika
2 tbsp tomato purée
salt
400g/14 oz can chopped tomatoes
6 tbsp plain yoghurt
chopped parsley, to garnish ·

Trim the lamb and cut into cubes. Heat the butter in a frying pan and brown the meat on all sides. Drain and put in a casserole dish. Add the onions to the pan and cook to soften. Sprinkle on the paprika and stir well, gradually adding the wine and the tomato purée. Season and pour over the lamb.

Add the tomatoes to the dish. Cover, bring to the boil and transfer to the simmering oven for about 2 hours, or the electric oven at 150°C. Just before serving, stir in the yoghurt and sprinkle with parsley.

Serves 6
....

TRADITIONAL GREEK MOUSSAKA

This must be the most well known of Greek dishes. Some people use cooked lamb instead of raw, but I prefer this cooked from scratch. Aubergines are usually used as the topping but if you prefer you can use sliced, part-cooked potatoes.

2 aubergines, sliced
salt
olive oil
1 large onion sliced
2 cloves garlic crushed
450g/1 lb minced lamb
400g/14 oz can chopped tomatoes
1 tbsp chopped fresh basil or 1 tsp dried oregano
freshly grated nutmeg
150ml/¼ pint red wine or stock
pepper

SAUCE:

300ml/½ pint milk
25g/1 oz flour
25g/1 oz butter
salt and pepper
pinch ground cinnamon
1 egg, beaten

Place the sliced aubergines in a colander and sprinkle with salt. Leave for 30 minutes then pat dry. Heat a tablespoon of olive oil in a frying pan and fry the aubergines on both sides until golden brown. Drain on kitchen paper. You will probably need to add more oil with each batch.

Heat a little oil in a flameproof casserole and sauté the chopped onion. Add the garlic and meat, and brown the meat well. Add the tomatoes, basil or oregano, nutmeg, wine or stock, and salt and pepper. Cover, bring to the boil and then place in the simmering oven for 1–2 hours. For an electric cooker, simmer over

a low heat for the same time. The meat should be tender and the sauce thick.

In an ovenproof dish make a base layer of half the fried aubergines. Spoon on the cooked lamb and top off with the remaining aubergines.

For the sauce, put the milk, flour, butter, and salt and pepper in a saucepan, and whisk over a medium heat until a smooth, glossy sauce is formed. Whisk in the cinnamon and the egg. Pour over the top of the aubergines and bake in the roasting oven with the shelf on the bottom set of runners, for about 15 minutes until the sauce is fluffy and golden brown. If using an electric oven, bake at 180°C.

Serves 4

LAMB AND APRICOT CASSEROLE

The addition of the apricots make a rich lamb casserole. The saffron, although expensive, adds a golden colour and a distinctive flavour. Creamed potatoes or saffron rice go well as accompaniments.

2 tsp ground cumin
1 tsp cloves
1 sprig fresh thyme
4 cloves garlic, crushed
175ml/6 fl oz fresh orange juice
3 tbsp olive oil
1.5kg/3 lb 5 oz boneless diced lamb
175g/6 oz dried apricots
75g/3 oz raisins
1 tsp saffron strands
300 ml/¹/₂ pint dry sherry
90ml/3 fl oz wine vinegar
3 tbsp flour
450ml/³/₄ pint light stock
salt and pepper

In a large bowl mix together the cumin, cloves, thyme, garlic, orange juice and olive oil. Add the diced lamb and stir well. Cover and leave in the fridge to marinate overnight or for at least 3 hours. In a basin combine the apricots, raisins, saffron, sherry and vinegar. Marinate overnight or for at least 3 hours. Skim the oil from the marinade and heat this in a frying pan. Brown the meat well and transfer to a casserole. Stir the flour into the remaining oil in the pan and cook for about a minute. Whisk in the stock to make a smooth sauce. Add the fruit to the casserole and pour the marinade into the sauce in the pan. Season with salt and pepper. Pour over the meat and fruit in the casserole dish. Bring the casserole to the boil on the simmering plate and bubble for 5 minutes. Transfer to the simmering oven, or the electric oven at 150°C for 3–4 hours.

Serves 8

MADRAS LAMB CURRY

This curry can easily be made for a crowd. It is best made the day before it is needed and reheated for the best flavour.

1 small fresh coconut or 50g/2 oz desiccated coconut
2 fresh red chillies, seeded and chopped
3 tsp paprika
2.5cm/1 inch piece fresh ginger root, chopped
6 cloves garlic
3 tsp ground coriander
2 bay leaves
cinnamon stick
6 cloves
1 tsp cumin seeds and 1 tsp poppy seeds
3 tbsp vegetable oil
2 onions, chopped
1kg/2 lb 4 oz stewing lamb, diced
3 tomatoes, peeled and chopped

If using desiccated coconut, soak half of it in some water. Take half the fresh coconut or the remaining desiccated coconut and place in a blender or food processor with 225ml/8 fl oz water. Whizz and then strain. Reserve the liquid.

Strain the soaked dried coconut or take the remaining half of the fresh coconut and put in the processor with the chillies, paprika, ginger, garlic, coriander, bay leaves, cinnamon stick, cloves, cumin seeds and poppy seeds. Grind together to make a paste. Add a little water if necessary. Heat a flameproof casserole with the oil and sauté the onion. Stir in the spice paste and fry over a low heat for about 15 minutes, stirring and adding 2–3 tablespoons of water if necessary to prevent burning. Add the diced meat and fry to brown all over. Add the tomatoes and cook again for 4–5 minutes to soften the tomatoes. Season with salt and add the reserved coconut liquid. Cover, bring to the boil and transfer to the simmering oven for 4-5 hours. If cooking on an electric hob, it may be necessary to add some water during cooking to prevent drying out.

Serves 6

LAMB CURRY WITH FRIED SPICES

....

This is more a flavoursome dish than a hot curry. If you like heat in your curry replace the green chillies with hot red ones. Don't be put off by the long list of ingredients – there is nothing outlandish!

2 tbsp vegetable oil
7.5cm/3 inch stick cinnamon
3 bayleaves
10 peppercorns
6 cloves
1 large onion, finely chopped
5cm/2 inch piece fresh ginger root, finely chopped
2 cloves garlic, crushed
2 green chillies, seeded and chopped
1 tsp salt
1kg/2 lb 4 oz boneless lamb, cut into chunks
¹/₂ tsp ground turmeric
1 ¹/₂ tsp ground coriander
1 tsp chilli powder
1 tsp garam masala
200g/7 oz can chopped tomatoes
4 tbsp plain yoghurt
1 cup water
fresh coriander leaves, to garnish

Heat the oil in a roomy frying pan and fry first the cinnamon and bay leaves, then the peppercorns and cloves. Add the onions and sauté until soft and lightly coloured. Add the ginger, garlic, chillies and salt, stir well and continue to cook for a further 2–3 minutes. Transfer to a flameproof casserole dish.

Brown the lamb in the hot pan and then add the turmeric, coriander, chilli powder and garam masala, and stir well. Add the tomatoes and the water if the mixture seems dry.

Add the lamb to the casserole dish and bring to the boil over a gentle heat. Transfer to the simmering oven for 3–4 hours. If you are using an electric oven, add at least another cup of water and cook at 150°C for 2 hours. Stir the yoghurt into the lamb and warm through. Garnish with coriander leaves and serve.

Serves 6

SHEPHERD'S PIE

This is a dish often made with left–over cooked meat, but I like to make a shepherd's pie with slowly cooked fresh minced lamb. The slow cooking ensures that the meat is always tender. Top it off with fluffy mashed potatoes.

1 tbsp oil or dripping
1 onion, finely chopped
450g/1 lb minced lamb
1 tbsp flour
salt and pepper
150ml/¹/₄ pint brown stock
1 tsp chopped parsley
1 tsp Worcestershire sauce
450g/1 lb potatoes, cut into even sized chunks
25g/1 oz butter
1–2 tbsp milk

Heat the oil in an ovenproof casserole and fry the onion until softening. Stir in the lamb and fry until evenly browned. Stir in the flour and cook for 1–2 minutes. Season with salt and pepper, and add the stock, parsley and Worcestershire sauce. Cover and bring to the boil then transfer to the simmering oven for 1–2 hours.

Place the potatoes in a saucepan, add a pinch of salt and about 2.5cm/1 inch of water. Bring to the boil and boil for 1 minute. Drain the water off, cover and transfer to the simmering oven for 40–60 minutes. When soft, drain again and mash with the butter and milk.

Remove the meat from the oven and pour into an ovenproof dish. Top with the mashed potatoes. Bake in the middle of the roasting oven for 30–40 minutes until golden brown on the top and piping hot.

Serves 6

LANCASHIRE HOTPOT

This is a traditional English stew taking its name from the deep pot in which it was always made. Although it has simple ingredients the combination of meat on the bone and long, slow cooking gives a delicious homely flavour. The kidneys add richness but may be left out if they are not to your liking.

1 tbsp vegetable oil or dripping
8 middle neck lamb chops
4 lamb kidneys, cored and sliced
1kg/2 lb 4 oz potatoes, sliced
2 onions, sliced
salt and pepper
300ml/^{1}/$_2$ pint light stock

Heat the oil or dripping in a frying pan and fry the chops and kidneys over a high heat until golden brown.

Put a layer of potatoes in the bottom of a deep ovenproof dish, layer on some of the onion and then some of the fried meat. Continue layering up, seasoning as you go. Finish with a layer of potatoes. Pour over the stock. Cover and cook in the simmering oven for 4–6 hours. Thirty minutes before serving, remove the lid and transfer to the roasting oven to brown the top of the potatoes.

For the electric oven, cook for 2–3 hours at 160°C, Remove the lid and raise the temperature to 220°C for the last 30 minutes.

Serves 4

SPICED LEG OF LAMB

The spices add a flavoursome skin to the lamb, without being overpowering. This method of cooking gives you delicious vegetables all in one dish along with the gravy. You may want to serve a green vegetable and baked or roast potatoes with the lamb.

2 tsp ground coriander
1 tsp ground cumin
1 tsp paprika
1 tsp salt
¹/₂ tsp freshly ground black pepper
¹/₂ tsp ground ginger
1.3kg/3 lb leg lamb
2 tbsp oil
1 large carrot, sliced
1 onion, sliced
2 celery stalks, sliced
150ml/¹/₄ pint stock
1 tsp tomato purée

Mix the spices together and rub into the leg of lamb. Place on a plate and leave in the fridge to marinate overnight.

In a large frying pan, heat the oil and soften the carrot, onion and celery. Drain the vegetables and transfer to the small roasting tin. Brown the meat all over in the hot fat – do not let it become too brown or the spices will taste bitter. Place the meat on the vegetables. Combine the stock and tomato purée, and pour round the vegetables.

Slide the tin on the second set of runners from the bottom of the roasting oven and roast the lamb for 30 minutes, then transfer to the simmering oven for 2 ¹/₂ hours. If using an electric oven, cover with foil or a lid and cook at 160°C for 2 hours. The juices may be thickened slightly (see page 21) or served as they are.

Serves 6

CARDAMON LAMB

·····································

This is a gentle spicy lamb dish – not at all hot – but if you like you can increase the chilli powder.

35 green cardamon pods
6 tbsp vegetable oil
2 tsp freshly ground black pepper
1 tsp ground turmeric
1 tsp chilli powder
1kg/2 lb 4 oz lamb meat, diced
150g/5 oz thick plain yoghurt
2 tsp ground coriander
3 tomatoes, peeled and chopped
salt

Place the cardamon pods in a processor or grinder and grind until fairly fine. Mix with a little water to make a paste.

Heat the oil in a flameproof casserole, add the cardamon paste and the pepper. Stir-frying the meat for 2-3 minutes. Add the turmeric, chilli powder and coriander, and stir in the meat. Cook over a medium heat, stirring, to cook the spices and prevent the meat sticking to the pan.

Add the yoghurt, tomatoes and a seasoning of salt. Stir well and then add about 300ml/½ pint water. Cover, bring to the boil and then transfer to the simmering oven for 4–5 hours. This may be done for 3 hours in an electric oven at 160°C.

······························ **Serves 6** ······························

SPRING LAMB

....

This is a delicate lamb casserole that suits the combination of spring lamb and baby new vegetables. If you can, choose small, evenly sized carrots as these will make the finished dish more attractive.

4 double cutlets of lamb
salt and pepper
25g/1 oz butter
2 small onions, finely sliced
300ml/¹/₂ pint stock
225g/8 oz young carrots, scraped and trimmed
450g/1 lb small, new potatoes, scrubbed

Trim the chops, cutting off excess fat. Season with salt and pepper. Melt the butter in a frying pan and brown the cutlets. Place in a shallow casserole dish. Add the onions to the hot frying pan and cook until soft. Add to the meat and pour on enough stock to barely cover the cutlets.

Place the prepared potatoes and carrots round the meat. Cover and slowly bring to the boil. Transfer to the simmering oven and cook for 1¹/₂–2 hours until the meat and vegetables are cooked. If using the electric oven, cook at 170°C for 1 ¹/₂ hours.

Serves 4
....

NAVARIN OF LAMB

This is a springtime recipe incorporating tender spring vegetables that give a bright appearance to the finished dish.

3 tbsp olive oil
1kg/2 lb 4 oz boned shoulder of lamb, cut into large dice
100g/4 oz each onion, celery and carrot, cut into large dice
2 cloves garlic, crushed
2tbsp tomato purée
1 tbsp flour
150ml/¼ pint dry white wine
2 bay leaves
sprig of fresh thyme
1L/1 ¾ pints stock
100g/4 oz small carrots
150g/6 oz small new potatoes
1 tbsp caster sugar
25g/1 oz butter
100g/4 oz each of asparagus and French beans
salt and pepper

Heat the oil in a large frying pan and brown the meat in batches, transferring to a casserole. Fry the onion, celery and carrot until softening. Add the garlic, tomato purée and flour and stir well. Slowly add the wine and bubble until reduced by half. Add to the lamb along with the bay leaves, thyme and stock. Bring to the boil over a gentle heat and transfer to the simmering oven for 1½–2 hours, or at 150°C in the electric oven. Trim the small carrots and new potatoes. Put the sugar, butter, 150ml/5 fl oz water, carrots and potatoes in a saucepan. Bring to the boil and transfer, uncovered, to the simmering oven for 15 minutes. At this point the vegetables should be glazed.

Remove the lamb from the casserole to a plate. Discard the bay leaves and thyme. Purée the gravy and vegetables left in the casserole. Cook the beans and asparagus in a little fast-boiling water for 3–4 minutes. Combine the lamb and sauce, and season to taste. Add the potatoes, carrots, beans and asparagus.

Serves 6

LAMB COUSCOUS

....

This is a complete meal on a plate — however there is some last-minute work to be done! Adding the vegetables to the lamb and preparing the couscous will take about 30 minutes. Harissa is a spicy Moroccan chilli paste, available from most supermarkets and specialist food shops.

50g/2 oz butter
1 clove garlic, crushed
2 onions, chopped
1 red chilli, chopped
2 bay leaves
1 tsp ground cumin
1/2 tsp freshly ground black pepper
1/2 tsp ground ginger
1 cinnamon stick
450g/1 lb lamb, diced
400g/14 oz can chick-peas, drained
2 each carrots, small turnips and courgettes,
trimmed and quartered.
4 tomatoes, peeled and quartered
1 small aubergine, diced
3 tbsp chopped fresh coriander
3 tbsp chopped parsley
450ml/³/4 pint light stock
225g/8 oz couscous
50g/2 oz butter
salt and pepper
harissa, (optional)

Heat the butter over a low heat in a flameproof casserole and stir in the garlic, onions, chilli, bay leaves, cumin, pepper, ginger and cinnamon stick. Fry for 1-2 minutes. Add the lamb and chick-peas, and enough water to half cover the lamb. Cover and bring to the boil. Transfer to the simmering oven, or electric oven at 150°C, for 2 hours. Add the prepared vegetables and herbs to the lamb, bring to the boil again and return to the simmering oven for a further 20-30 minutes until the vegetables are cooked.

Bring the stock to the boil in a saucepan, stir in the couscous. Remove from the heat and cover. Stand for 20 minutes,then stir in the butter. Check seasoning and serve with the lamb. To add a little more heat and an authentic flavour, accompany this wonderful dish with a small bowl of harissa,

Serves 4

CIDER PORK WITH APPLES

Pork and apples always go well together. Use red-skinned apples to add colour to the finished dish.

1kg/2 lb 4 oz pork shoulder, cut into large dice
1 tbsp seasoned flour
3 tbsp oil
2 large onions, cut into eighths
300ml ¹/₂ pint cider
300ml ¹/₂ pint light stock
salt and pepper
2 red-skinned eating apples

Toss the meat in the seasoned flour. Heat the oil in a frying pan and brown the meat in batches. Transfer to a casserole dish. Add the onions to the frying pan, gently fry until softening and golden brown. Add to the meat.

Stir the cider and stock into the frying pan, season with salt and pepper and bring to the boil, scraping up all the residue from the base of the pan. Pour over the meat in the casserole. Place the casserole on the simmering plate, cover and bring to the boil. Transfer to the simmering oven and cook for 1 hour.

Quarter and core the apples and add to the casserole and cook for another 30–40 minutes until the meat and apples are tender, but not falling apart. For the electric oven cook at 160°C for the same time.

Serves 6

SOMERSET CIDER HOTPOT

I like to make this with pork, but veal or even pieces of bacon joint also work well with this meal-in-a-pot.

675g/1 lb 8 oz pork, cubed
1 tbsp seasoned flour
2 tbsp vegetable oil
675g/1 lb 8 oz potatoes, thickly sliced
450g/1 lb leeks, trimmed and sliced
salt and pepper
450ml/³⁄₄ pint Somerset cider
2 tbsp tomato purée

Coat the meat with seasoned flour. Heat the oil in a frying pan and brown the meat all over.

Lay some potatoes in the base of the casserole dish and then a layer of leeks, seasoning each layer with salt and pepper. Put in the browned meat, then more leeks and finish with a layer of potatoes.

Mix together the cider and tomato purée, and pour over the potatoes. Cover, bring to the boil and transfer to the simmering oven for 3–4 hours. Remove the lid and brown off in the roasting oven for 30 minutes. For the electric oven cook at 170°C for 2 hours, then raise the heat to 190°C and remove the casserole lid for 30 minutes to brown the potatoes.

Serves 4

NEW ORLEANS CAJUN PORK

This is a flavoursome way to cook pork that has the added bonus of looking attractive on the plate with a range of bright colours. It is best served with couscous or rice.

1 kg/2 lb 4 oz diced shoulder pork
4 green chillies, seeded and finely chopped
4 cloves garlic, crushed
¼ tsp cayenne pepper
1 tbsp Cajun seasoning
2 tbsp vegetable oil
2 large onions, peeled and cut into wedges
1 red pepper, seeded and cut into large squares
1 yellow pepper, seeded and cut onto large squares
400g/14 oz can plum tomatoes
150ml/¼ pint chicken stock
2–3 sprigs fresh thyme
salt and pepper

Place the pork, chillies, garlic, cayenne and Cajun seasoning in a bowl and mix well. Cover and leave in the fridge overnight.

Heat the oil in a frying pan and fry the pork until a deep golden brown. Transfer to a casserole dish. Add the onions and peppers to the frying pan and cook for 5 minutes until just starting to colour and soften. Add to the pork. Stir in the remaining ingredients and season with salt and pepper.

Place the casserole on the simmering plate and bring gently to the boil. Transfer to the simmering oven for 3–4 hours or in the electric oven at 130°C for the same time.

Serves 6

PORK WITH HONEY AND APRICOTS

....

Pork and fruit always work well together. Dried apricots add a delicious flavour and texture – slightly Middle Eastern. Serve with couscous or mashed potatoes.

1kg/2 lb 4 oz boneless pork, diced
2 tbsp seasoned flour
2 tbsp vegetable oil
2 onions, chopped
100g/4 oz dried apricots
salt and pepper
2 tbsp honey
600ml/1 pint light stock
1 cinnamon stick

Toss the pork in the seasoned flour. Heat the oil in a frying pan and brown the prepared meat. Transfer to a casserole dish.

Add the onions to the hot frying pan and sauté until softening and a pale golden colour. Stir in the apricots, salt and pepper to taste, honey and stock. Bring to the boil and pour over the meat. Add the cinnamon stick and cover. Bring to the boil. Place in the simmering oven for 3–4 hours or at 160°C for 2 hours.

....
Serves 6
....

PORK WITH RED WINE AND PRUNES

The addition of prunes, redcurrant jelly and red wine gives a rich sauce to this pork casserole. Serve with mashed potatoes to absorb the rich gravy.

2kgs/4 lb 8 oz boneless shoulder of pork, diced
2 tbsp seasoned flour
2 tbsp vegetable oil
2 onions, sliced
1/2 bottle red wine
300ml/1/2 pint light stock
225g/8 oz redcurrant jelly
225g/8 oz ready-to-eat prunes
a few sprigs thyme
2–3 sage leaves

Toss the pork in the seasoned flour. Heat the oil in a frying pan and brown the meat in batches. Transfer each batch to a large casserole dish.

Cook the onions in the frying pan until softening, pour in the wine and bring to the boil. Add the stock and redcurrant jelly, stirring to dissolve the jelly, and add the prunes. Pour the hot liquid over the meat in the casserole and add the herbs. Bring to the boil and transfer to the simmering oven for 2 hours.

Serves 8

PORK CASSEROLE WITH HERB DUMPLINGS

1kg/2lb 4oz pork shoulder steaks
2 tbsp seasoned flour
2 tbsp vegetable oil
2 onions, 2 large carrots, sliced
4 celery stalks, chopped
600ml/1 pint light stock
1 bouquet garni
salt and pepper

DUMPLINGS:

100g/4 oz self-raising flour
100g/4 oz fresh breadcrumbs
100g/4 oz shredded suet
salt and pepper
$^1/_2$ tsp, dried mixed herbs or 1 tbsp chopped fresh mixed herbs

Toss the pork in the seasoned flour. Heat the oil in a frying pan and brown the meat on all sides. Transfer to a casserole dish. Add the onion, celery and carrot to the pan and sauté until softening. Pour in the stock and bring to the boil. Pour the mixture over the meat and add the bouquet garni and a seasoning of salt and pepper. Cover and bring to the boil. Transfer to the simmering oven for about 4 hours, or the electric oven at 160°C for 2 hours.

Prepare the dumplings. In a mixing bowl mix together the flour, breadcrumbs, suet, salt, pepper and herbs. Blend together with enough cold water to make a stiff dough. Shape into 12 dumplings. Place the dumplings on the top of the meat, so that the base is sitting in the gravy. Transfer the casserole to the bottom set of runners of the roasting over or raise the temperature of the electric oven to 180°C, and cook for a further 20–30 minutes.

Serves 6

SCRUMMY SAUSAGES

Most children like sausages, pasta and tomato sauce, so this way of cooking sausages and serving with pasta is usually a winner.

3 tbsp olive oil
2 large onions, finely chopped
2 cloves garlic, crushed
1 large red chilli, seeded and finely chopped
2 x 400g/14 oz cans chopped tomatoes
1 tsp sugar
salt and pepper
8 thick sausages
3 tbsp seasoned flour
pasta shapes, to serve

In a flameproof casserole heat 1 tablespoon of the oil and fry the onion, garlic and chilli until soft. Add the tomatoes, sugar, and salt and pepper. Bring to the boil and transfer, uncovered, to the simmering oven for at least an hour until a thick sauce has formed.

Skin the sausages and cut each one into three. Roll each portion into a ball and roll to coat in the flour. Heat the remaining 2 tablespoons of oil in a frying pan and brown the sausage balls until golden brown all over. Add to the tomato sauce, bring to the boil and then return to the simmering oven for 30 minutes. Serve with pasta shapes.

Serves 6

BOSTON BAKED BEANS

This is a classic American recipe, although the beans in this recipe bear no resemblance to the canned variety! The treacle gives a dark colour and a distinctive sweetness. Sausages browned in a frying pan can be added for the last hour to make a substantial one-pot meal.

225g/8 oz dried cannellini beans
bouquet garni
500ml/18 fl oz vegetable stock
450g/1 lb belly pork
1 leek, finely sliced
1 carrot, sliced
1 onion, quartered
2 tbsp black treacle
2 tsp strong mustard
2 tbsp soft brown sugar
salt and pepper

Pick over the dried beans and place in a bowl. Cover with cold water and soak overnight. Drain, rinse and put in a saucepan. Add the bouquet garni and enough stock to just cover the beans. Cover, bring to the boil, then transfer to the simmering oven for 1 hour until just tender. Drain, reserving the cooking water.

Chop the pork into large cubes and put half in the base of a casserole dish. Add the beans and the prepared vegetables and then the remaining meat. Mix together the treacle, mustard and sugar, add to the casserole and season to taste. Pour in enough of the bean cooking water to almost cover the ingredients. Cover and gently bring to the boil on the simmering plate, then transfer to the simmering oven for 6 hours. If using an electric oven cook at 120°C for the same time. Check the seasoning before serving.

Serves 4–6

VEAL GOULASH

Stewing veal is readily available in butchers shops and supermarkets. It makes a tasty stew.

1kg/2 lb 4 oz stewing veal
1 tbsp flour
25g/1 oz butter
1 tbsp vegetable oil
1 onion, sliced
2 carrots, sliced
150ml/¹/₄ pint white wine
1 tbsp paprika
¹/₂ tsp cayenne pepper
1 tbsp tomato purée
450ml/³/₄ pint light stock
salt

Toss the meat in the flour. Heat the butter and oil in a frying pan and brown the meat all over. Transfer to a casserole dish.

Add the onion and carrots to the pan, sauté, then add to the meat. Pour the wine into the hot pan and scrape off all the residue from the base of the pan. Stir in the paprika, cayenne, tomato purée and the stock, and bring to the boil. Lightly season with salt.

Pour the liquid over the meat, cover, bring to the boil and transfer to the simmering oven for 2–3 hours or the electric oven at 160°C for 1¹/₂–2 hours. Check seasoning before serving.

Serves 6

CASSEROLE OF VEAL

....

350g/12 oz shoulder of veal, boned and cut into strips
75g/3 oz butter
2 onions, sliced
3 carrots, sliced
1 clove garlic, crushed
25g/1 oz seasoned flour
300ml/¹/₂ pint veal or chicken stock
4 tomatoes, peeled, seeded and chopped
4 celery stalks, chopped
salt and pepper

Toss the veal in the seasoned flour. Heat the butter in a frying pan and brown the meat in this. Drain and transfer to a casserole dish. Add the onions and carrots to the hot butter and fry until softening. Add the garlic and any remaining flour. Cook for 1–2 minutes, then gradually stir in the stock. Bring to the boil, then add the tomatoes and celery. Simmer for 1–2 minutes and add to the veal. Season to taste, cover and bring back to the boil. Transfer to the simmering oven for 2 hours. If using an electric oven cook at 160°C.

....
Serves 4
....

OSSO BUCO

This is a classic Italian dish using veal that is cooked gently in a tomato sauce. The sauce becomes rich from the slow cooking and the marrow in the bones. Serve with a rissotto or creamy mashed potatoes.

4 pieces osso buco shin of veal
salt and pepper
1 tbsp plain flour
2 tbsp olive oil
1 onion, finely chopped
1 clove garlic, crushed
1 carrot, diced
1 celery stalk, finely sliced
1 leek, finely sliced
50g/2 oz peeled and diced celeriac
1 tbsp chopped basil
2 tomatoes, peeled and chopped
2 tbsp tomato purée
150ml/^{1}/$_4$ pint dry white wine
600ml/1 pint beef stock

Season the osso buco with salt and pepper, and lightly dust with flour. Heat the oil in a frying pan and brown the meat well on both sides. Transfer to a casserole dish large enough to take all the meat pieces in one layer.

Sauté the onion, garlic, carrot, celery, leek and celeriac for a few minutes in the hot pan, until the vegetables are softening. Stir in the basil, tomatoes, tomato paste and the wine. Stir well and bubble until reduced by half. Add the stock and again boil well, then pour over the osso buco. Cover, return to the boil, then place in the simmering oven, or the elecric oven at 160°C, for 3–4 hours, until the veal is tender and the sauce is thick. Check the seasoning before serving.

Serves 4

VEGETABLE CURRY

....

This is a warming winter dish best made when there is a plentiful supply of root vegetables. Other vegetables can be substituted for those listed but do not overload the variety otherwise you will lose the individual flavours. Cut the vegetables large enough to give a good appearance and bite to the curry.

2 cloves garlic, peeled
2.5cm/1 inch cube fresh ginger root, grated
2 tsp each coriander seeds and cumin seeds
1 tsp each mustard seeds and cardamom seeeds
10 cloves
1 stick cinnamon, about 7.5cm/3 inches
1 tsp cayenne pepper, 1 tsp ground turmeric
75g/3 oz clarified butter, ghee or vegetable oil
400ml/14 fl oz can coconut milk
juice 1 lemon
2 large parsnips, chopped
¹/₂ small cauliflower, broken into florets
100g 4 oz button mushrooms, wiped
a large head broccoli, cut into portions
4 potatoes, cut into chunks
1 large onion, sliced
4 carrots, chopped
1 tsp salt

Put the garlic and ginger in a mortar or small processor and grind to make a paste. Grind the whole spices to a powder, then mix with the cayenne and turmeric. In a flameproof casserole heat the butter and sauté the onion, garlic and ginger until the onion is golden brown. Add the salt and spices, and cook for 1–2 minutes. Add the carrots, coconut milk and lemon juice. Bring to the boil and then add the parsnips, cauliflower, mushrooms and potatoes. Cover and transfer to the simmering oven for about 1 hour, until the vegetables are tender, but not mushy. Remove the casserole from the oven and stir in the broccoli. Cook quickly to retain the bright colour. Taste and adjust the seasoning.

....
Serves 6
....

PROVENÇAL BEAN STEW

This is a two-stage dish, in that the beans need to be cooked before adding to the remaining ingredients. This makes a good main course dish served with crispy salad and good bread to mop up any juices.

350g/12 oz haricot beans, soaked overnight
2 tbsp olive oil
1 onion, sliced
1 red pepper, seeded and sliced
1 green pepper, seeded and sliced
2 cloves garlic, crushed
400g/14 oz can chopped tomatoes
2 tbsp tomato purée
salt and pepper
12 black olives, pitted
10 basil leaves, shredded

Drain the beans, place in a flameproof casserole and cover with cold water. Cover and bring to the boil, then transfer to the simmering oven for 2–3 hours. Drain and set aside.

In the casserole, heat the oil and sauté the onion, red and green peppers and garlic until softening, but not brown. Add the tomatoes, tomato purée and some salt and pepper. Stir in the cooked beans, bring gently to the boil and transfer to the simmering oven for 1–1¹/₂ hours. Stir in the olives and sprinkle with basil.

Serves 4

ACCOMPANIMENTS

ACCOMPANIMENTS

Casseroles and stews out of the simmering oven deserve a good accompaniment. The easiest, of course, are jacket potatoes, deservedly one thing that new Aga owners rave about, with their crispy skins and fluffy insides.

If the main dish has a lot of gravy choose a starchy accompaniment that will absorb some of the juices. Rice goes well with curries, and couscous with fruity Mediterranean dishes, but they can, of course, be used with other dishes or even as salads. The list is endless, here are just a few ideas.

POLENTA

....

This is an everyday food in Northern Italy, so with the increase in Italian foods being eaten in this coutry it is not surprising to see polenta widely available in the supermarkets. Served hot and wet it is a good accompaniment to casseroles and stews. Allowed to set and then grilled or fried, it goes well with drier food and salads. If you buy ready-cooked or quick-cook polenta then follow the instructions on the packet.

250g/9 oz polenta
1.2L/2 pints water
salt and pepper
100g/4 oz butter
75g/3 oz freshly grated Parmesan cheese (optional)
olive oil

Pour the polenta into a jug. Measure the water into a saucepan and bring to the boil. Transfer to the simmering plate and stir in the polenta in a steady stream, beating well. Cook over a gentle heat, stirring vigorously and frequently until the polenta comes away from the sides of the pan. Season with salt and pepper.

Stir the butter, and cheese if using, into the hot polenta at once. Serve.

If you wish to serve the polenta grilled or fried, pour on to a shallow plate or baking tray and allow to cool and set. To grill or fry, cut into portions and brush with olive oil. Then grill or fry until golden brown.

....
Serves 4
....

DUMPLINGS

Small dumplings are used to finish off stews and casseroles. Once the dumplings have been added to the casserole move the dish to the roasting oven for the final cooking time. They are a delicious way of soaking up the gravy.

HERB AND HORSERADISH DUMPLINGS FOR BEEF STEWS:

100g/4 oz self-raising flour
100g/4 oz white breadcrumbs
50g/2 oz shredded suet
2 tbsp chopped mixed herbs
2 tsp horseradish sauce
salt and pepper
1 or 2 eggs, beaten

Mix together the flour, breadcrumbs, suet and herbs. Add the horseradish, salt and pepper. Stir in enough beaten egg, to make a soft dough. Divide into 16 dumplings. Place on top of the stew for the last 30 minutes of the cooking time.

PARSLEY DUMPLINGS FOR VEAL, LAMB AND CHICKEN:

175g/6 oz fresh breadcrumbs
75g/3 oz shredded suet
2 tbsp chopped parsley
grated rind ¹/₂ lemon
salt and pepper
1 or 2 eggs, beaten

Mix together the breadcrumbs, suet, parsley, lemon rind, and salt and pepper. Stir in enough beaten egg to make a soft dough. Put spoonfuls of the dough on top of the casserole for the last 15–20 minutes.

SUET DUMPLINGS:

These are always associated with beef stews. Ring the changes with flavourings such as mustard, chopped mint or sorrel.

225g/8 oz plain flour
¹/₂ tsp baking powder
salt
100g/4 oz shredded suet

Sieve the flour, baking powder and salt into a basin. Mix in the suet and bind together with cold water to make a stiff dough. Shape into 16 dumplings and cook for 20 minutes on top of the casserole.

....

RED CABBAGE WITH APPLE

Red cabbage is delicious with rich meats such as pork or game. I like any left-overs cold as a salad.

1 small red cabbage
1 cooking apple, peeled, cored and thickly sliced
1 small onion, thinly sliced
25g/1 oz butter
salt and pepper
1 tbsp redcurrent jelly (optional)

Shred the cabbage finely — this can be done either in a food processor or with a sharp knife. Place in a flameproof casserole with the apple, onion and butter. Season with salt and pepper and toss well to mix. Cover and heat gently on the simmering plate until the butter has melted. Place in the simmering oven for about 2 hours. If you like, add a tablespoon of redcurrant jelly before serving.

Serves 4-6

POTATO AND APPLE MASH

....

This is a favourite mashed potato recipe to go with sausages and pork.

To every 450g/1 lb of potatoes use one cooking apple. Peel the potatoes and cut into large chunks. Peel, quarter and core the apples. Put together in a saucepan with about 2.5cm/1 inch water. Cover and bring to the boil on the boiling plate, and boil for 1 minute. Drain and replace the lid. Transfer to the simmering oven for about an hour or until the potatoes are soft enough to mash. Drain off any excess moisture and mash the apples and potatoes with butter until smooth. Season with salt and pepper. Grate a red-skinned apple, leaving the skin on, and fold into the mash. This gives an attractive appearance.

....

MASHED SWEDE

....

Swede can be very dull as a boiled vegetable, but cooked this way it is delicious.

Peel the swede, cut into large chunks and place in a saucepan with 2.5cm/1 inch water and a pinch of salt. Cover and bring to the boil on the boiling plate and boil for 1 minute. Drain the water from the pan and replace the lid. Transfer to the simmering oven for 1–1$^{1}/_{2}$ hours. When the swede is soft enough to mash, drain the water. Mash or purée the swede with plenty of butter and a generous grating of nutmeg. Taste and season with salt if needed.

....

GARLIC MASHED POTATOES

A favourite with my publisher! Olive oil can be used to mash the potatoes, but personally I prefer butter.

450g/1 lb maincrop potatoes
salt
4 cloves garlic, peeled
50g/2 oz butter or 2–3 tsp olive oil
pepper

Place the potatoes in a saucepan with about 2.5cm/1inch water, a good pinch of salt and the garlic cloves. Cover and bring to the boil. Boil for 1 minute and then drain off the water. Re-cover and place the pan in the simmering oven for 40–60 minutes until the potatoes are soft enough to mash. Drain off any excess moisture and mash the potatoes and garlic with the butter and some pepper.

Serves 4

PARSNIP PURÉE

Parsnips are one of my favourite winter vegetables. Those baby ones in the super-market in the summer have no flavour, so keep this as a winter dish to go with hearty roasts and warming casseroles.

Peel and cut the parsnips into large chunks. Place in a saucepan with about 2.5cm/1 inch water and a pinch of salt. Cover and bring to the boil on the boiling plate. Boil for 1 minute and then drain off the water. Cover and transfer to the simmering oven until the parsnips are soft enough to mash. This may take 1–1 ¹/₂ hours, depending on the age of the parsnips. Drain any excess moisture and then mash or purée the parsnips with butter, salt and pepper, a pinch of cinnamon and a little chopped parsley.

CELERIAC PURÉE

Although this has the flavour of celery it is a totally different vegetable. Unless you grow your own it tends to be fairly expensive, so I usually mix it with potatoes, which absorb the strong flavour well.

Peel and cut into large chunks the potatoes and celeriac – about equal quantities of each vegetable. Place in a saucepan with 2. 5cm/1 inch water and a pinch of salt. Bring to the boil on the boiling plate and boil for 1 minute before draining off the water. Cover and transfer to the simmering oven until the vegetables are soft enough to mash – about 1 hour. Drain off any excess moisture and then mash with a good knob of butter, some hot milk or cream, and a seasoning of salt and pepper.

FLAGEOLET BEAN SALAD

These dried green beans are probably the family favourite. They are a good ingredient for a mixed bean salad. This recipe can have salami pieces added to make the salad a meal in itself.

250g/8 oz dried flageolet beans, soaked overnight
salt and pepper
1 clove garlic, crushed
6 tbsp olive oil
3 tbsp white wine vinegar
1/4 tsp French mustard
pinch sugar
1 spring onion, finely chopped

Drain the beans and cover with fresh water in a flameproof casserole. Bring to the boil and transfer to the simmering oven for 1 1/2–2 hours, until cooked but not mushy. Drain and transfer to a serving dish.

Place the remaining ingredients in a jam jar and shake well. Pour over the drained beans and stir well.

BUTTER BEAN VINAIGRETTE

For many years butter beans were my least favourite bean having had too many mushy ones at school! This recipe converted me, and my family likes them too!

250g/8 oz butter beans, soaked overnight
3 tbsp olive oil
1 tbsp wine vinegar
salt and pepper
4 spring onions, finely chopped
1 clove garlic, crushed
chopped parsley, to garnish

Rinse the beans and place in a flameproof casserole. Cover with water and bring to the boil. Cover and place in the simmering oven for $1^{1}/_{2}$–2 hours until the beans are cooked, but not mushy. Drain and transfer to a serving dish.

Place the oil, vinegar, and salt and pepper in a clean jam jar. Shake well and pour over the warm, beans. Add the onions and garlic and mix well, taking care not to break up the beans. Leave until cold, then sprinkle with chopped parsley to serve.

Serves 4–6

PUY LENTILS

The advantage of lentils is that they need no soaking. These little brown lentils have a lovely texture and nutty flavour. Serve this dish warm or cold as an accompaniment to other dishes or in a salad selection.

225g/8 oz Puy lentils, washed thoroughly
6 cloves garlic, unpeeled and cut in half
juice of 1 lemon
3 tbsp olive oil
2 tbsp chopped herbs, whatever is handy
salt and pepper

Place the lentils and garlic in a saucepan or flameproof casserole. Cover with water and bring to the boil. Cover and transfer to the simmering oven for 30–60 minutes until soft but still with some bite. Drain the lentils and discard the garlic. Mix together the lemon juice and olive oil, and pour over the lentils. Stir in the herbs and season with salt and pepper. Serve warm or cold.

Serves 6

COUSCOUS

....

Couscous is a staple from North Africa. The grain is made from semolina. It can be eaten as a salad or as an accompaniment for meat stews.

225g/8 oz couscous
450ml/³/₄ pint stock

Bring the stock to boil in a saucepan, then stir in the couscous. Remove from the heat and stand at the back of the Aga, covered. Leave to stand for 20 minutes. Fork through to fluff up and, if liked, stir in some butter, olive oil or vinaigrette dressing, depending upon what you are serving the couscous with.

....

SPICY CHICK-PEAS

Chick-peas are a useful source of protein for vegetarians, but they also make a delicious vegetable dish, either hot or cold.

225g/8 oz dried chick-peas, soaked overnight in cold water
2.5cm/1 inch cube fresh ginger root
1 green chilli, seeded and chopped
2 cloves garlic, peeled
2 tbsp vegetable oil or ghee
1 onion, chopped
¹/₂ tsp cumin seeds, crushed
1 tsp coriander seeds, crushed
1 tsp chilli powder
¹/₂ tsp ground turmeric
4 tomatoes, peeled and chopped
juice ¹/₂ lemon
salt and pepper

Drain the chick-peas and place in a large pan. Cover with water and bring to the boil, covered. Transfer to the simmering oven for about 2 hours, until tender. Drain and reserve the liquid.

Pound the ginger, chillis, and garlic together to make a paste, using either a mortar or processor. Heat the oil in a frying pan and sauté the onion until soft. Stir in the chilli paste, the crushed seeds, the chilli powder and turmeric, and cook for 1–2 minutes. Add the tomatoes and lemon juice. Stir into the chick-peas and moisten with some of the cooking liquid if the beans seem dry. Heat through in the simmering oven for 30 minutes, check the seasoning and serve hot or cold.

Serves 6

RATATOUILLE

This Mediterranean vegetable stew has been popular for years. The fashion now is to have a barely cooked selection of vegetables, but I still like a slow cooked stew. This is a versatile dish to serve on its own, as an accompaniment to simply-cooked food, topped with cheese, cold as a salad or as a basis of a vegetable lasagne.

3 tbsp olive oil
2 cloves garlic, crushed
1 bay leaf
sprig of rosemary or thyme
2 onions, chopped
2 peppers, colour of choice, seeded and cut into large dice
2 courgettes, trimmed and sliced
450g/1 lb firm, ripe tomatoes, peeled, seeded and roughly chopped
1 aubergine, trimmed and cut into large dice
salt and pepper

Heat the oil in a flameproof casserole along with the garlic and herbs. Sauté the onions in the oil until softening but not browning. Drain and put to one side.

Now sauté the remaining vegetables in turn, then return them all to the pan, season and toss. Cover, heat through and transfer to the simmering oven for 1 hour until the vegetables are cooked but not mushy.

Serves 4–6

JACKET POTATOES

....

Scrub the potatoes well and cut a cross on one side of the potato. Place the potatoes on the oven shelf in the roasting oven and bake for 1–1½ hours until crisp on the outside and fluffy in the middle. If using an electric oven bake at 180°C.

The fillings listed below can be used either as a topping for the potatoes or the inside can be scooped out and mixed together with the chosen filling.

FILLINGS:

grated hard cheese such as Cheddar, Red Leicester or Gruyère

slices of soft Brie mixed with chopped walnuts

poached smoked haddock or salmon mixed with soured cream and parsley

canned tuna fish, chopped chives and mayonnaise, mashed lightly together

soured cream and crushed garlic

fromage frais

butter and crispy fried bacon

butter and crispy fried onion rings

sliced mushrooms sautéd in butter and mixed with thick yoghurt

blue cheese crumbled into soured cream

ACCOMPANIMENTS

PUDDINGS

PUDDINGS

....

The best puddings cooked slowly are steamed puddings – here the variety is almost endless. A quickly prepared pudding can be made from a basic all-in-one sponge mixture and topped off with jam or syrup. Here I am giving one or two slightly more exotic variations on the everyday steamed pudding. Remember that if you are not ready to serve the pudding at the time planned it will not spoil – 1–2 hours extra cooking is quite safe! The steaming on the simmering plate or in the roasting oven is important to get a light, fluffy sponge. Allow extra cooking time if you know your simmering oven cooks very slowly.

I have also added a selection of recipes for other puddings which benefit from slow cooking. Meringues in particular are suitable for slow cooking in the Aga's simmering oven. They can even be left in overnight!

....

STEAMED ORANGE SPONGE

A light orange sponge served with an orange sauce. If you can, use frozen concentrated orange juice for a deep flavour.

100g/4 oz butter, softened
125g/4¹/₂oz castor sugar
2 eggs, beaten
1 egg yolk
200g/7 oz self-raising flour
finely grated rind 1 orange
150ml/¹/₄ pint concentrated orange juice
Orange Sauce (see below) or cream, to serve

Cream together the butter and the sugar. Beat together the eggs and yolk, and beat into the creamed mixture. Fold in the flour and orange rind, then gently mix in the orange juice to make a soft dropping consistency. Grease a 1.2L/2 pint pudding basin and carefully spoon in the mixture. Cover with greaseproof paper and either pleated foil or a fitting lid. Stand in a large saucepan. Pour in boiling water to come half-way up the sides of the basin. Cover, bring to the boil and simmer for 30 minutes, then transfer to the simmering oven for 2¹/₂-3 hours.

ORANGE SAUCE:

600ml/1 pint orange juice or 300ml/¹/₂ pint
concentrated orange juice
25–50g/1–2 oz sugar
1 tsp cornflour
1 tbsp cold water

If using ordinary orange juice, boil to reduce to 300ml/¹/₂ pint. Add sugar to taste. Mix together the cornflour and water, and whisk into the hot orange juice. Cook for 3–4 minutes, whisking, until a good sauce is formed.

Serves 6

STEAMED FRUIT PUDDING

This is a suet pastry pudding into which you can put any fruits you have available such as apples, plums, blackcurrants. It is a perfect pudding to prepare in the morning and serve in the evening as the moisture in the fruit means that the pudding needs a lot of cooking.

275g/10 oz plain flour
100g/4 oz castor sugar
1 tsp baking powder
150g/5 oz shredded suet
200ml/7 fl oz milk
450g–900g/1–2 lb prepared chosen fruit
sugar, to taste

Sieve the flour, castor sugar and baking powder into a bowl and stir in the suet. Bind together with enough milk to make pliable dough. Cut off two-thirds and roll into a circle. Use to line a 1.2L/2 pint pudding basin. Fill with fruit and sugar to taste. Roll the remaining pastry to make a lid. Seal well. Cover with greaseproof paper and foil, and stand in a large saucepan. Pour enough boiling water into the pan to come half-way up the sides of the basin. Bring to the boil on the simmering plate and simmer for 30 minutes. Transfer to the simmering oven for 5 hours or longer, depending on the fruit.

Serves 6–8

MARMALADE PUDDING

I find this a good way to use up left-over homemade marmalade from the previous year when I have made a new batch in January. This recipe also uses a lot of oranges, which are plentiful and juicy then. Serve with the whisky sauce.

5 oranges (some are used in the sauce)
175g/6 oz butter, softened
175g/6 oz castor sugar
3 eggs, beaten
175g/6 oz self-raising flour
6 tbsp marmalade

SAUCE:

75g/3 oz butter
75g/3 oz castor sugar
3 tbsp whisky
2 tbsp marmalade

Finely grate the rind from one orange. Squeeze the juice from three oranges. Peel the remaining two and cut the flesh into segments.

Cream together the butter and sugar. Add the grated orange rind and beat in the eggs. Fold in the flour, marmalade and 2 tablespoons of orange juice. Spoon 4 tablespoons of marmalade into a 1.2L/2 pint greased pudding basin, and top with the sponge mixture. Cover with greaseproof paper and either foil or a fitting lid. Place in a large saucepan and pour in enough boiling water to come half-way up the sides of the basin. Cover, bring to the boil and simmer for 30 minutes. Transfer to the simmering oven for 2–2 $^{1}/_{2}$ hours.

To make the sauce, melt together the butter and the sugar over a gentle heat. Cook gently until golden brown. Add the whisky and the remaining orange juice and cook until syrupy. Off the heat, stir in the marmalade and the orange segments. Turn out the pudding and serve with the whisky sauce.

Serves 6–8

PLUM DUFF

This pudding was my father's favourite, preferrably served with rice pudding!

225g/8 oz plain flour
2 tsp baking powder
1 tsp mixed spice
75g/3 oz castor sugar
100g/4 oz shredded suet
175g/6 oz raisins
300ml/¹/₂ pint milk

Sieve together the flour, baking powder, spice and sugar. Stir in the suet and raisins. Blend in the milk and place in a buttered 1.2L/2 pint pudding basin. There should be enough room for the pudding to rise. Cover with greaseproof paper and foil or a lid. Stand in a deep saucepan and pour in enough boiling water to come half-way up the sides of the basin. Cover, bring to the boil and simmer for 30 minutes. Transfer to the simmering oven for 3–4 hours.

Serves 6

RICH RICE PUDDING

....

This recipe was sent to me by Mrs Peters in Lancashire. It is truly delicious. I find this best to make in an Aga cast-iron dish that will go on the hot plate, into the oven and look good at the table.

60g/2 ¹/₂ oz butter
40g/1 ¹/₂ oz caster sugar
90g/3 ¹/₂ oz pudding rice
1.2 Litre/2 pint full cream milk
¹/₂ vanilla pod or ¹/₂ tsp vanilla essence

Put the butter in the cast-iron dish and place on the simmering plate to melt. Stir in the sugar and cook until the mixture becomes toffee-like in consistency, but not brown, Add the rice and stir well until it is sticky and coated. Add the milk and the vanilla pod, if using. (Add vanilla essence later.) Squash the pod to remove the seeds while bringing the mixture gently to the boil. Remove the pod or add essence at this point.

When the milk is boiling, transfer to the simmering oven for 4 hours, or the electric oven at 110°C. This is best served warm, not hot straight from the oven.

Serves 6–8, depending upon appetite!
....

RICE PUDDING

....

This has to be one of the Aga-owners easiest puddings. This recipe will only work with full-cream milk! A spoonful of cream will make this special.

75g/3 oz pudding rice
50g/2 oz sugar
1.2L/2 pint milk
25g/1 oz butter

Put the rice in a buttered 1.7L/3 pint ovenproof dish. Sprinkle on the sugar and pour in the milk. Dot with butter.

Put the oven shelf on the floor of the roasting oven. Put in the pudding for 30–40 minutes until the milk is hot and skin has formed. Transfer to the simmering oven for 4–5 hours. For the electric oven bake at 150°C for 3 hours.

....
Serves 8
....

GOLDEN BREAD PUDDING

Use stale croissants or brioche to give a slightly special bread and butter pudding.

4 large croissants, cut in half
50g/2 oz butter
3 eggs
300ml/¹/₂ pint milk
300ml/¹/₂ pint single cream
4 tbsp golden syrup

Spread the croissants with the butter and lay in a buttered ovenproof dish. Mix the eggs, milk and cream together and strain over the croissants. Drizzle over the golden syrup. Stand the dish in a roasting tin and pour round boiling water. Put the oven shelf on the floor of the roasting oven, put in the pudding and bake for 30 minutes. Transfer to the simmering oven for 1¹/₂–2 hours. For the electric oven bake at 150°C for 1 hour.

Serves 4–6.

CHICHESTER PUDDING

I started my teaching career in Chichester and have fond memories of that beautiful city. I hope you enjoy the pudding!

6 eggs, separated
75g/3 oz sugar
600ml/1 pint milk
pinch ground cinnamon
175g/6 oz fresh white breadcrumbs

Beat the egg yolks and sugar together in a basin. Warm the milk and cinnamon together in a saucepan and pour over the egg mixture, whisking. Place the breadcrumbs in a bowl and strain the custard on to them. Whisk the egg whites until stiff and gently fold into the custard mixture. Do not over-mix as there should be a marbled effect.

Pour into a 1.2L/2 pint buttered oven–proof dish. Stand in the roasting tin. Pour boiling water round the dish and bake for 20 minutes in the roasting oven, then transfer to the simmering oven for 2 hours, until set. For the electric oven cook at 170°C for 1 hour.

Serves 6

HAZELNUT MERINGUES

These meringues are good sandwiched together with cream and fruit or even a little melted chocolate. You can make individual meringues or make two layers to sandwich together for a pudding.

225g/8 oz caster sugar
1 tsp cornflour
4 egg whites
175g/6 oz hazelnuts, toasted and finely chopped

FILLING:

150ml/¹/₄ pint double cream, whipped
225g/8 oz raspberries or strawberries, optional
50g/2 oz plain chocolate, melted

Line the cold shelf with baking parchment or Bake-O-Glide. Mix the sugar and cornflour. Whisk the egg whites until stiff but not dry. Continue whisking and add the sugar one teaspoonful at a time. Fold in the hazelnuts.

Spoon two circles of meringue mixture on the prepared cold shelf. Slide into the middle of the simmering oven for 4–5 hours. If using the electric oven bake at 75°C for 4–5 hours. Leave to cool.

Place one circle of meringue on a serving plate, spread over the whipped cream and scatter over the fruit, if using. Drizzle over some of the melted chocolate. Place the second meringue on top and drizzle over the remaining chocolate.

Serves 6

BROWN SUGAR MERINGUES

The brown sugar gives a rich colour and caramel flavour. If you want to store these, make sure they are dried out well.

100g/4 oz caster sugar
100g/4 oz soft brown sugar
3 egg whites
whipped cream

Weigh the sugars and mix together. Line the cold shelf with baking parchment or Bake-O-Glide. Whisk the egg whites until thick and fluffy, but not dry. As you continue to whisk, add the sugar 1 teaspoonful at a time.

Pipe or spoon individual meringues on to the prepared cold shelf. Slide into the middle of the simmering oven for at least 4 hours or even overnight. If using the electric oven bake at 75°C for 3-4 hours. Store in an airtight container until needed. Sandwich together with whipped cream.

Note: to prevent 'weeping' of the meringues do not whisk in the sugar too quickly. Do not dry out more than one tray at a time.

Makes about 16

DRIED FRUIT COMPÔTE

This is such an easy pudding to make. It is delicious served hot or cold. The range of dried fruits available mean that you can ring the changes from something simple like apple rings, prunes and apricots to more exotic combinations with peaches and mangoes.

450g/1 lb assorted dried fruits
grated rind and juice of 1 orange
1 tbsp whisky

Soak the dried fruits for 2–3 hours in cold water. (If the fruits have been in your cupboard sometime they may need longer soaking.)

Place in a flameproof casserole with the soaking water, orange juice and rind, and whisky. The fruits should be just covered by liquid, add more water if necessary. Cover and bring gently to the boil.

Transfer to the simmering oven and allow to cook for 1–2 hours, until the fruits are cooked but not losing their shape. Serve warm or cold.

Serves 6

PEARS IN RED WINE

This is a good way to cook under-ripe pears. The cooking time will vary according to the ripeness of the fruit.

300ml/¹/₂pint red wine
225g/8 oz sugar
2 cloves or 1 cinnamon stick
1 kg/2 lb 4 oz pears, peeled, halved and cored
flaked almonds, to decorate

Pour the wine into a saucepan, add the sugar and the cloves or cinnamon. Dissolve the sugar over gentle heat, bring to the boil and then add the prepared pears. Cover and transfer to the simmering oven for 1¹/₂–2 hours. Sprinkle with almonds and serve warm with cream.

Serves 6–8.

BAKED APPLES

An autumn favourite. Experiment with different fillings.

cooking apples, one per person
sugar
butter
golden syrup

Core the apples and make a horizontal slit in the skin round the middle. Stand in an ovenproof dish. Put a little sugar into each apple. Dot each apple with butter and drizzle over a little golden syrup. Put 1–2 tablespoons water in the bottom of the dish. Put the shelf on the floor of the roasting oven and put in the apples for 20 minutes. Then transfer to the simmering oven for 1¹/₂-2 hours until soft.

CRÈME BRULÉE

This is a rich, creamy dessert best made the day before it is needed because it does require chilling. Six ramekin dishes should fit into the small roasting tin.

500ml/1 pint double cream
1 vanilla pod or 1 tsp vanilla essence
4 egg yolks
50g/2 oz caster sugar

Pour the cream into a saucepan and add the vanilla pod (add vanilla essence later). Stand on the simmering plate to warm through. Place the egg yolks into a basin with the sugar and whisk until thick and fluffy. Remove the vanilla pod from the cream and pour the cream onto the egg mixture, whisking. If using vanilla essence, whisk this in at this point. Strain into a jug.

Stand six ramekins in the small roasting tin and pour the custard into each one. Pour hot water into the roasting tin to come half-way up the sides of the ramekins. Slide into the simmering oven, on the second set of runners from the top and cook for 3–4 hours until set. If using an electric oven bake at 150°C for 1¹/₂–2 hours. The mixture will still be slightly wobbly even when cooked. Cool overnight.

CARAMEL TOPPING:

Unless you have a very hot domestic grill, it is difficult to get a successful brulée topping. Some people use a blow torch! I make caramel and pour over. Place 100g/4 oz granulated sugar in a saucepan and stand over a low heat. Warm to dissolve the sugar, but try not to stir. When the sugar has melted keep an eye on the pan as the sugar burns easily. Heat the pan until the sugar turns a pale caramel colour and then drizzle the caramel over the chilled custards. Serve. Do not stand for too long or the caramel will soften.

Serves 6

'WHICKED' WALNUT PUDDING

....

This is possibly the richest and most calorific pudding I make! The name comes from my children, 'whicked' meaning exceptionally good!

150g/5 oz butter
175g/6 oz soft brown sugar
300ml/¹/₂ pint double cream
100g/4 oz dates, chopped
¹/₂ tsp bicarbonate soda
1 egg
100g/4 oz self-raising flour
50g/2 oz walnuts, chopped

In a small saucepan warm together 75g/3 oz of the butter and 100g/4 oz of the sugar. Stir in the cream. Bring to the boil and bubble fast for a few minutes to make a fudge sauce. Put the dates in a basin and cover with 150ml/¹/₄ pint of boiling water and the bicarbonate of soda. Leave to stand for 10 minutes to soften the dates.

Cream together the remaining 50g/2 oz butter and 50g/2 oz sugar. Beat in the egg and the date mixture. Fold in the flour and the walnuts. Do not worry if the mixture looks curdled at this stage!

Pour 2–3 tablespoons of the fudge sauce into the base of a greased 1.2L/2 pint pudding basin. Spoon in the pudding mixture. Cover with greaseproof paper and foil or a lid. Stand the basin in a deep saucepan and pour in enough boiling water to come half-way up the sides of the basin. Cover and bring the water to the boil. Simmer for 30 minutes, then transfer to the simmering oven for 2–3 hours. Turn out and serve with the remaining fudge sauce.

....
Serves 6
....

CHUTNEYS

CHUTNEYS

The Aga is the perfect cooker for making chutney. By using the simmering oven for the long slow cooking, the vinegar smell will disappear up the chimney and not invade the house. There is also no need to constantly watch the pot for burning. Long, slow cooking of chutney improves the flavour.

Again, a good-sized preserving pan is useful, and as the chutney is not boiled rapidly the pan can be about two-thirds full. Jar lids need to be coated to prevent corrosion by the vinegar. Warm in the simmering oven before filling. Brown and white sugar can be used. Dark brown sugar will give a darker chutney and a rich flavour. Similarly dark malt vinegar will colour the chutney, while for a lighter pickle you can use white wine vinegar.

I know it is tempting to try the chutney as soon as it is made, but it really needs 4–6 weeks for the flavours to develop and the strong vinegar flavour to mellow. Use jars that are scrupulously clean and lids that are acid-resistant.

CRANBERRY CHUTNEY

....

Most people associate cranberries with Christmas, and this chutney makes a very welcome Christmas gift. Frozen cranberries are available all year round, so make this at any time to go with poultry.

700g/1 lb 8 oz cranberries
300ml/¹/₂ pint wine vinegar
225g/8 oz sultanas
grated rind and segments from 3 oranges
100g/4 oz sugar
15g/¹/₂ oz salt
2 tsp ground cinnamon
2 tsp ground allspice

Wash and pick over the cranberries. Place in a preserving pan or large saucepan with the remaining ingredients. Stand on the simmering plate and heat gently to dissolve the sugar. Stir well, cover and bring to the boil. Transfer to the simmering oven and cook for 1–1¹/₂ hours until thick. Pour into jars, cover and label.

Makes about 1kg/2 lb 4 oz
....

CHUTNEYS

APRICOT CHUTNEY

....

This can be made at any time of year if your supplies are running low. This is particularly good with cold pork and pork pies.

450g/1 lb dried apricots, chopped
450g/1 lb sultanas
4 large onions, chopped
12 fresh red chillies, seeded and chopped
900ml/1¹/₂ pints malt vinegar
450g/1 lb brown sugar
25g/1 oz salt

Use either a mincer or a processor for this. Mince the apricots, sultanas, onions and chillies together. Do not over-process. Place in a preserving pan with the vinegar, brown sugar and salt. Bring to the boil, transfer to the simmering oven and cook for 2–2¹/₂ hours until thick. Pour into jars, seal and label.

Makes about 1.8kg/4 lb
....

PLUM CHUTNEY

Make this when plums are plentiful or substitute rhubarb or damsons for the plums. Lovely with cold meat.

450g/1 lb onions, chopped
450g/1 lb cooking apples, peeled and cored
2kgs/4 lb 8 oz plums, halved and stoned
225g/8 oz sultanas
600ml/1 pint vinegar
600g/1 lb 8oz soft brown sugar
25g/1 oz salt
4 cloves
1 piece dried root ginger, bruised
1 tsp mustard seeds
2 black peppercorns

Place the onions and apples in a large preserving pan or saucepan. Add the plums, sultanas, vinegar, sugar and salt. Put the cloves, ginger, mustard seeds and peppercorns in a muslin bag and bury this in the mixture. Cover, place the pan on the simmering plate and bring slowly to the boil, stirring occasionally. When boiling well, remove the lid and place in the simmering oven for about 2 hours until the mixture is thick and jam-like. Pour into jars, seal and label.

Makes about 2.25kg/5 lb

BANANA AND DATE CHUTNEY

I make this after Christmas to use up left-over dates and bananas. The chutney will be dark and rich.

1kg/2 lb 4 oz bananas, peeled and sliced
500g stoned dates, chopped
1kg/2 lb 4 oz cooking apples, peeled, cored and chopped
grated rind and juice of 2 oranges
2 tsp mixed spice
2 tsp ground ginger
2 tsp curry powder
2 tsp salt
600ml/1 pint malt vinegar
450g/1 lb sugar

Place all the ingredients in a large saucepan or preserving pan and mix well. Stand on the simmering plate and slowly bring to the boil, stirring occasionally. Transfer to the simmering oven for 1¹/₂–2 hours, until thick.

Makes about 3kg/6 lb 8oz

DRIED FRUIT CHUTNEY

A store-cupboard chutney. Chop the fruits to whatever consistency you like. Allow time for the fruits to soak overnight.

225g/8 oz dried apricots, chopped
225g/8 oz dried peaches, chopped
600ml/1 pint wine vinegar
450g/1 lb cooking apples, peeled, cored and chopped
225g/8 oz raisins
100g/4 oz dates, chopped
2 onions, chopped
2 cloves garlic, crushed
1/2 tsp salt
1/2 tsp ground coriander
1/2 tsp ground cloves
1 tsp dry mustard powder
pinch cayenne pepper
675g/1 lb 8 oz soft brown sugar

Place the apricots and peaches in a bowl with the vinegar. Leave to stand overnight. Transfer the mixture to a preserving pan and bring to the boil. Add the apples, raisins, dates, and onions. Stir well. Add the remaining ingredients, bring to the boil and transfer to the simmering oven for 1½–2 hours until the mixture is thick. Pour into jars, cover and label.

Makes about 2.25kg/5 lb

GREEN TOMATO CHUTNEY

Green tomato chutney is a good enough reason to grow your own tomatoes — where else do you get green tomatoes for this lovely chutney?

450g/1 lb onions, chopped
2.25kg/5 lb green tomatoes, chopped
¹/₂ tsp salt
15g/¹/₂ oz pickling spice, tied in a muslin bag
600ml/1 pint malt vinegar
450g/1 lb sugar

Put the onions in a large saucepan or preserving pan with a little water and stand on the simmering place to cook until softening. Add the tomatoes, salt and pickling spice and half the vinegar. Bring to the boil and place in the simmering oven for about 1¹/₂-2 hours until thick. Remove the pickling spice. Now stir in the sugar and the remaining vinegar. Dissolve the sugar over medium heat and when bubbling return to the simmering oven for another hour, until the mixture is like thick jam. Pour into jars, seal and label.

Makes about 2.25kg/5lb

TOMATO SAUCE

I like this preserved tomato sauce instead of tomato ketchup. If you like a smooth sauce, purée the mixture after cooking. This is a sauce, not a thick chutney.

18 large tomatoes, peeled and chopped
6 large onions, chopped
600ml/1 pint vinegar
100g/4 oz sugar
2 scant tbsp salt

Place all the ingredients in a saucepan or preserving pan. Stand on the simmering plate and heat to dissolve the sugar. Bring to the boil and transfer to the simmering oven for about 2 hours. Bottle, seal and label.

COOKS' NOTES

COOKS' NOTES

COOKS' NOTES

COOKS' NOTES

COOKS' NOTES

COOKS' NOTES

INDEX

ACKNOWLEDGEMENTS

....

I have to thank all the Aga customers in Bath, Cardiff, Neath and Dorchester who kindly asked me for another book. They have been a tremendous encouragement. As usual, Jon Croft of Absolute Press, who seems to have faith in me, and Bron Douglas, my editor, who keeps me going through thick and thin, have been a great help.

A good friend, Marian Jones and her family have willingly eaten a variety of recipe tests and usually come back with complimentary comments!

My family bear the brunt of any new book being written. Hanna can now have her stir-fries and quick pastas that she was longing for in the middle of testing so many casseroles. Dominic and Hugo have suffered winter soups and steamed puddings as temperatures reached 28°C at the beginning of their much-needed summer holiday. My biggest thanks must be to Geoff, my husband, who encourages me all the way, even when I can't get on with the computer or a recipe fails.

Louise Walker
July, 1997